OSLO *MADE EASY*

Andy Herbach

Europe Made Easy
Travel Guides
www.eatndrink.com

Second edition 2020
ISBN: 9798606415779
–All Rights Reserved–

Acknowledgments

Contributor: Karl Raaum
Editor: Marian Modesta Olson
Additional Research: Erik and Erin Raaum
All photos from Shutterstock, Pixabay, Erin Raaum,
and Karl Raaum
Cover photo: Karl Raaum

ABOUT THE AUTHOR

Andy Herbach is the author of the *Eating & Drinking* series of menu translators and restaurant guides, including *Eating & Drinking in Paris, Eating & Drinking in Italy, Eating & Drinking in Spain and Portugal,* and *Eating & Drinking in Latin America.* He is also the author of several travel guides, including *Paris Walks, Europe Made Easy, Paris Made Easy, Amsterdam Made Easy, Berlin Made Easy, Barcelona Made Easy, French Riviera Made Easy, Provence Made Easy, Oslo Made Easy* and *Madrid Made Easy.* Andy is a lawyer and resides in Palm Springs, California.

You can e-mail him corrections, additions, and comments at eatndrink@aol.com or through his website at www.eatndrink.com.

TABLE OF CONTENTS

MAPS

Reviews for travel guides by Andy Herbach

•

"...an opinionated little compendium."
Eating & Drinking in Paris
~ New York Times

"Everything you need to devour Paris on the quick."
Best of Paris
~ Chicago Tribune

"an elegant, small guide..."
Eating & Drinking in Italy
~ Minneapolis Star Tribune

"Makes dining easy and enjoyable."
Eating & Drinking in Spain
~ Toronto Sun

"Guide illuminates the City of Light."
Wining & Dining in Paris
~ Newsday

"This handy pocket guide is all you need..."
Paris Made Easy
~ France Magazine

"Small enough for discreet use..."
Eating & Drinking in Paris
~ USA Today

"It's written as if a friend were talking to you."
Eating & Drinking in Italy
~ Celebrity Chef Tyler Florence

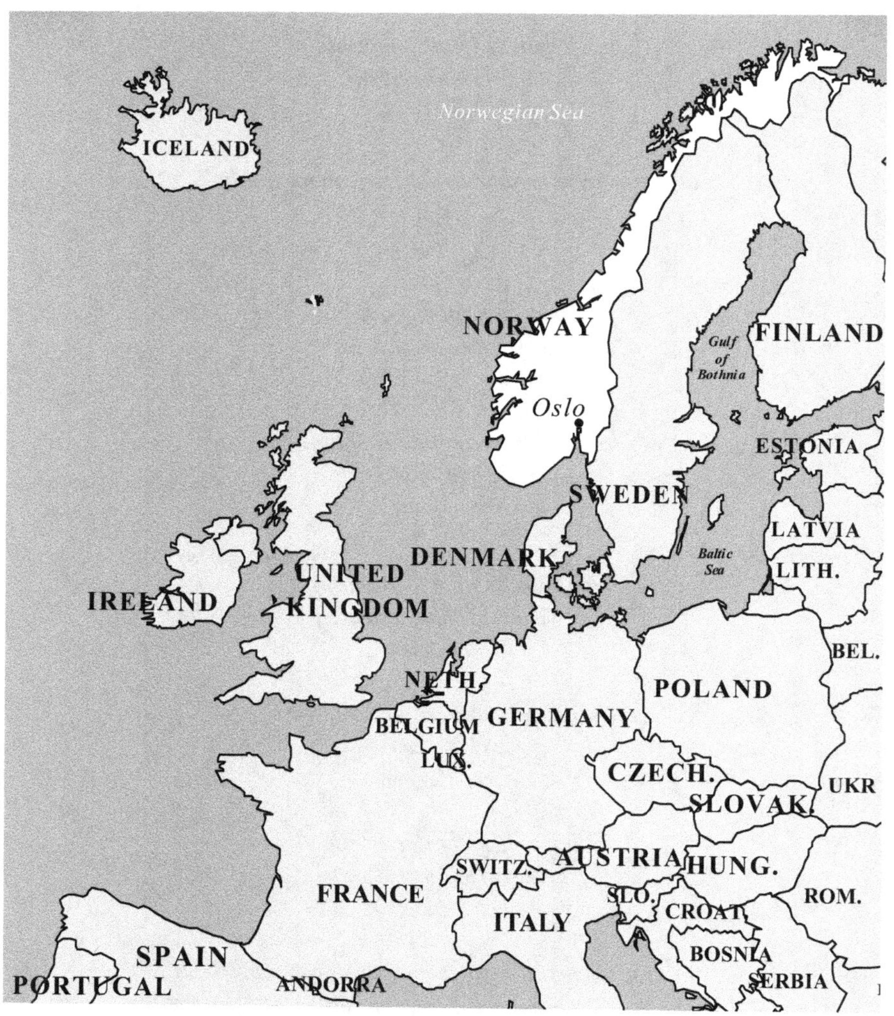
ICELAND
Norwegian Sea
NORWAY
FINLAND
Gulf
of
Bothnia
Oslo
ESTONIA
SWEDEN
LATVIA
Baltic
Sea
LITH.
DENMARK
UNITED
KINGDOM
BEL.
IRELAND
NETH.
POLAND
BELGIUM
GERMANY
LUX.
CZECH.
UKR
SLOVAK
SWITZ.
AUSTRIA
HUNG.
FRANCE
SLO.
ROM.
ITALY
CROAT
SPAIN
BOSNIA
PORTUGAL
ANDORRA
SERBIA

INTRODUCTION

Surrounded by forest and sea, magnificent **Oslo**, Norway's capital and largest city, has much to offer.

Oslo is evolving. So, even if you visited just a short time ago, you can be sure the city will have something new for you.

As the title says, our little guide will make your trip easy. You'll have access to Oslo's top sights right at your fingertips, including a sprawling Frogner Park, with works by Norway's greatest sculptor, and the Viking Ship Museum. And architectural gems are everywhere, from the historic Royal Palace, to the modern waterfront Opera House.

Tuck this book into your pocket and head out for a great day of sightseeing, with insider tips on cafes, restaurants, and shops.

If you have only a few days, we'll make it easy for you to truly experience Oslo. We'll also take you outside the city to experience some of Norway's other great destinations, including Bergen, and the fabulous fjords.

So forget those large, bulky travel books. This handy little guide to Oslo is all you need to make your visit enjoyable, memorable—*and easy*.

Oslo Overview

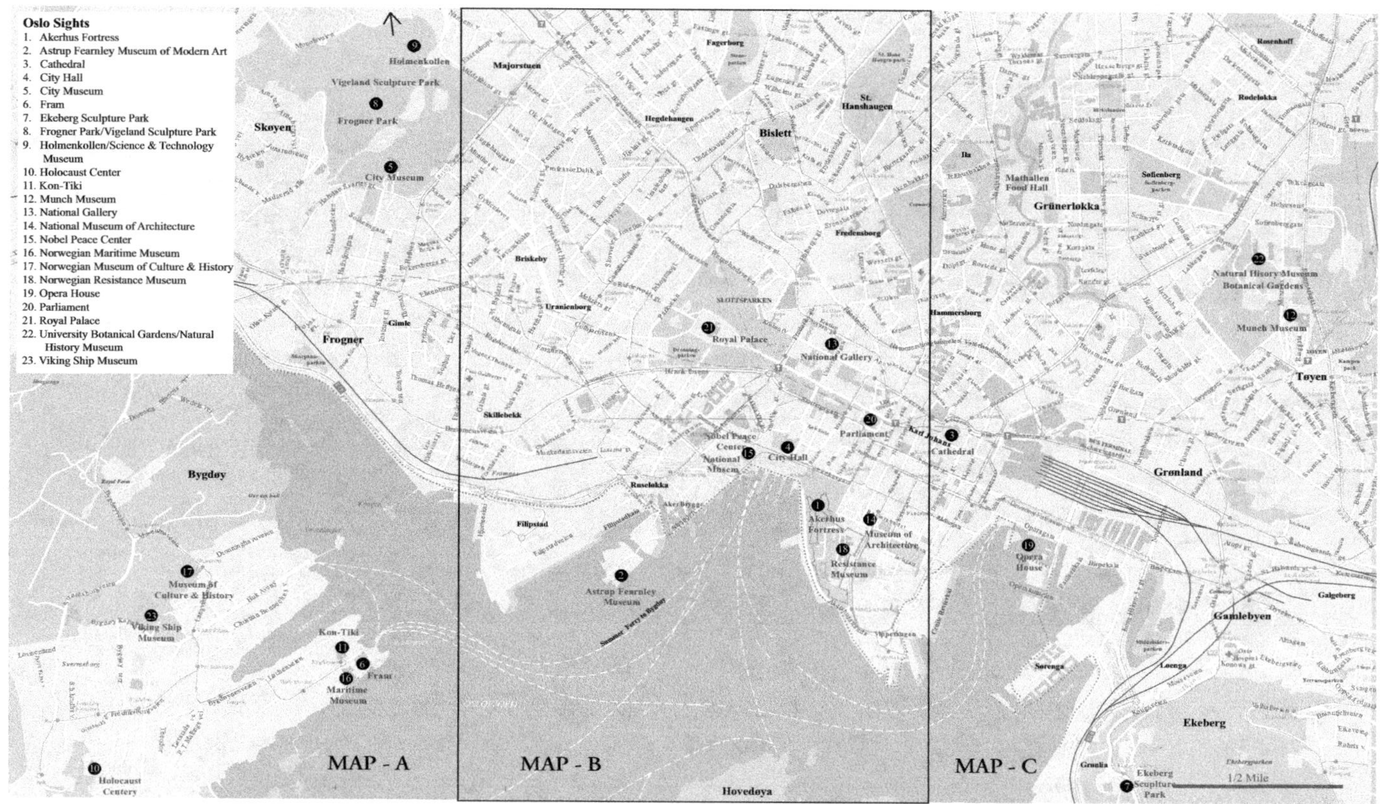

Oslo Sights

1. Akerhus Fortress
2. Astrup Fearnley Museum of Modern Art
3. Cathedral
4. City Hall
5. City Museum
6. Fram
7. Ekeberg Sculpture Park
8. Frogner Park/Vigeland Sculpture Park
9. Holmenkollen/Science & Technology Museum
10. Holocaust Center
11. Kon-Tiki
12. Munch Museum
13. National Gallery
14. National Museum of Architecture
15. Nobel Peace Center
16. Norwegian Maritime Museum
17. Norwegian Museum of Culture & History
18. Norwegian Resistance Museum
19. Opera House
20. Parliament
21. Royal Palace
22. University Botanical Gardens/Natural History Museum
23. Viking Ship Museum

Oslo Map - A

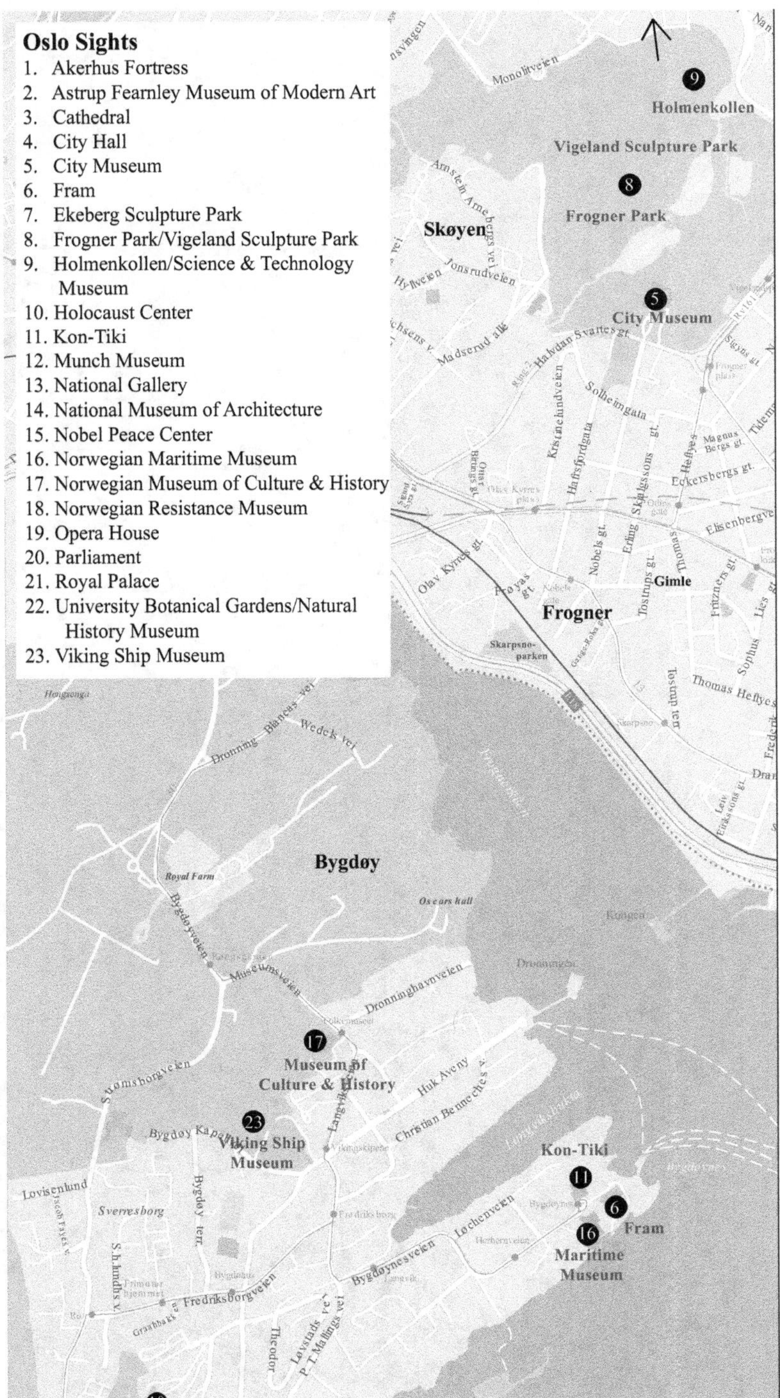

Oslo Map - B

Majorstuen
Fagerborg
Stens-parken
St. Hans Haugen park
Hegdehaugen
St. Hanshaugen
Bislett
Briskeby
Fredensborg
Uranienborg
SLOTTSPARKEN
21
Royal Palace
13
National Gallery
Skillebekk
Nobel Peace Center
National Museum
15
City Hall
4
20
Parliament
Karl Johan
Ruseløkka
1
Akerhus Fortress
14
Museum of Architecture
Filipstad
18
Resistance Museum
2
Astrup Fearnley Museum
Summer Ferry to Bygdøy
Vippetangen
Hovedøya

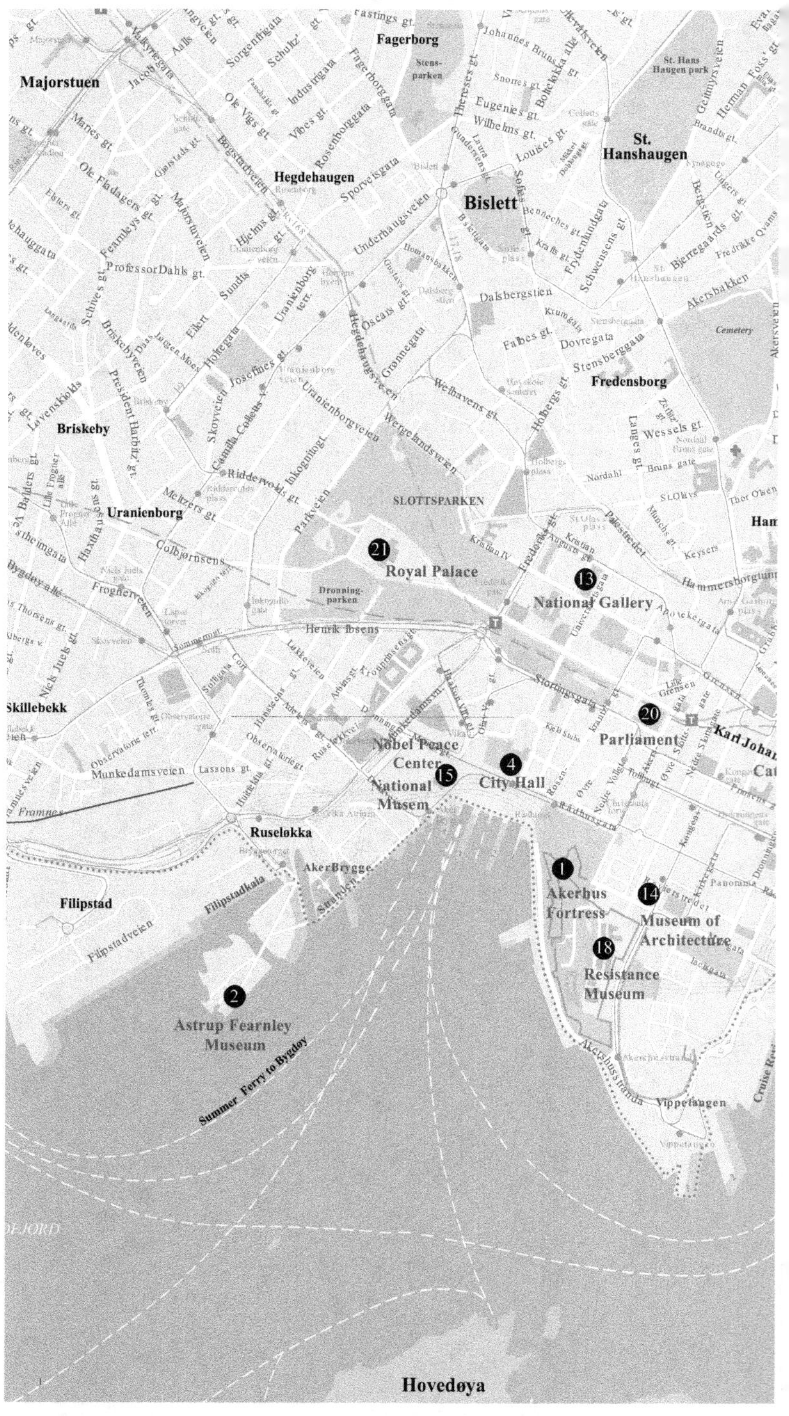

Oslo Map - C

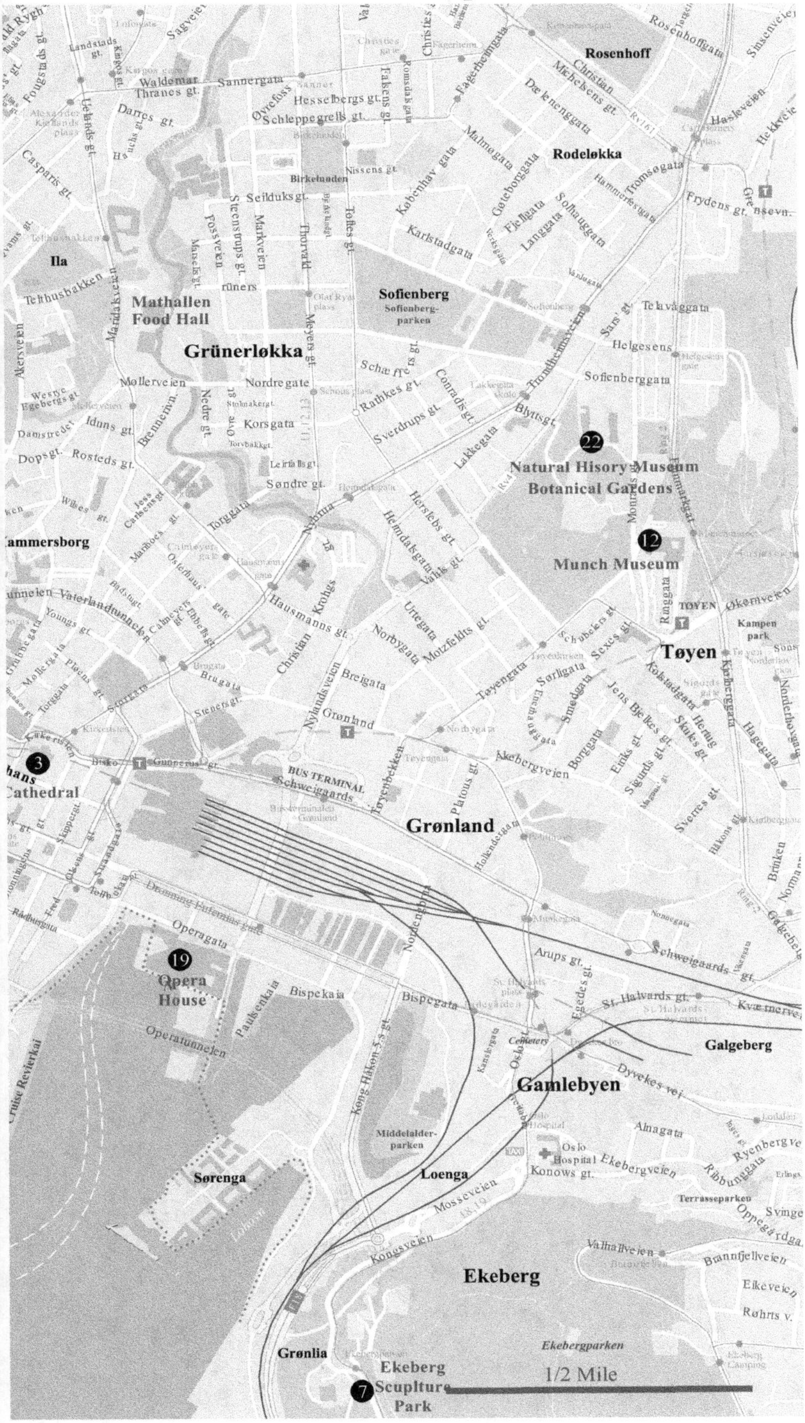
Rosenhoff
Rodeløkka
Ila
Mathallen
Food Hall
Grünerløkka
Sofienberg
Sofienberg-
parken
22
Natural Hisory Museum
Botanical Gardens
12
Munch Museum
Tøyen
Kampen
park
Grønland
BUS TERMINAL
3
Cathedral
19
Opera
House
Galgeberg
Gamlebyen
Middelalder-
parken
Sørenga
Loenga
Oslo
Hospital
Terrasseparken
Ekeberg
Ekebergparken
Grønlia
7
Ekeberg
Scuplture
Park
1/2 Mile

Norwegian Sea
Tromsø
Trondheim
NORWAY
FINLAND
Gulf
of
Bothnia
Lillehammer
Bergen
Oslo
ESTONIA
SWEDEN
LATVIA
DENMARK
Baltic
Sea
LITH.

OSLO TOP SIGHTS

- **Oslo City Hall (Oslo Rådhus)**
The Nobel Peace Prize is awarded in the impressive Central Hall decorated with murals depicting scenes from Norwegian history.

- **Opera House (Operahuset)**
The roof of this fantastic building angles to ground level (as if rising up from the water), creating a plaza that invites visitors to walk up to the top and enjoy panoramic views of the city.

- **National Gallery (Nasjonalgalleriet)**
Norway's largest collection of paintings, drawings, and sculptures. You'll find Munch's famous *The Scream* here.

- **Karl Johans Gate**
This grand boulevard runs from the Central Station to the stately Royal Palace, where you'll find the Cathedral and Parliament.

- **Frogner Park and the Vigeland Sculpture Park**
Home to an amazing sculpture collection.

- **Viking Ship Museum (Vikingskipshuset)**
One of the many museums found on the Bygdøy peninsula, it's home to three Viking ships dating back to the 9th century.

- **Norwegian Museum of Cultural History (Norak Folkemuseum)**
Historic buildings from throughout the country in an open-air museum.

- **Holmenkollen Ski Museum and Ski Jump**
Examine skiing history, experience the ski jump simulator, and take a zip line down to the base.

Opera House (Operahuset)

Royal Palace

Akershus Fortress
(Akershus festning)

Oslo City Hall (Oslo Rådhus)

Frogner Park and the
Vigeland Sculpture Park

Viking Ship Museum
(Vikingskipshuset)

Norwegian Museum of Cultural History
(Norsk Folkemuseum)

SIGHTS

There's something for everyone in this incredible city. You'll find fabulous architecture, great museums, and gorgeous parks. Get ready to experience one of Europe's best destinations!

We've arranged Oslo's top sights by city area. And we've also included excursions out of Oslo to experience some of Norway's interesting, scenic, and fun destinations!

Oslo
- Waterfront
- Bygdøy
- City Center
- West
- East/Grünerløkka/Grønland
- Holmenkollen

Excursions
- Lillehammer
- Oslofjord
- Bergen

Waterfront

- Akershus Fortress
- Astrup Fearnley Museum of Modern Art
- City Hall
- Nobel Peace Center
- Norwegian Resistance Museum
- Opera House

Oslo City Hall
(Oslo Rådhus)

Oslo City Hall is the city's administrative body and the seat of the City Council. Constructed between 1931 and 1950, the brown brick building features two towers. Every hour, the bell tower rings everything from classical music by Edvard Grieg to the Beatles. Carillon concerts are held on the first Wednesday of every month at 1pm.

Its art gallery contains works by Norwegian artists primarily from the early 20th century, featuring Norwegian culture and daily life. Every November, the City Hall is home to the Nobel Peace Prize ceremony. The Nobel Peace Prize Award presentation and other ceremonies at Oslo City Hall take place in the impressive Central Hall. Decorated with murals by artist Henrik Sørensens, titled *Administration and Festivity*, the works depict scenes from Norwegian history.

Pre-booked tours for groups of up to 30 persons are available all year. During June and July, guided tours are held at 10am, noon, and 2pm, in either Norwegian or English (but most in high season are in English). Bookings at omvisninger@rft.oslo.kommune.no or Tel. 23 46 12 00.

Info: Fridtjog Nansens plass. Tel. 23 46 12 00. Open 9am-4pm daily (until 6pm Jul and Aug). Admission: Free.

**Nobel Peace Center
(Nobels Fredssenter)**

The Nobel Peace Center celebrates the history of the Nobel Peace Prize. It's located in what used to be the Vestbanen railway station (near City Hall). Exhibits feature the Peace Prize laureates and their work, and tell the story of Alfred Nobel and the Peace Prize. The Center has permanent and temporary exhibitions on topics related to war, peace, and conflict resolution.

Info: 1 Brynjulf Bulls Pass. Tel. 48 30 10 00. Open daily 10am-6pm. Closed most Mon from Oct to Mar. Admission NOK150. Under 16 free. www.nobelpeacecenter.org.

Souvenirs

Norway Shop

This shop located next to City Hall sells Norwegian knitwear, gifts, and souvenirs. Everything sold here is made in Norway. *Info*: 9 Fridtjof Nansens Plass. Tel. 22 42 87 00. Open daily Mon-Sat 10am-6pm, Sun noon-6pm with extended hours in summer. www.norwayshop.com. Several other locations in Oslo, including on the city's main street at 8 Karl Johans gate. Tel 94 80 04 10. Open daily 9am-9pm.

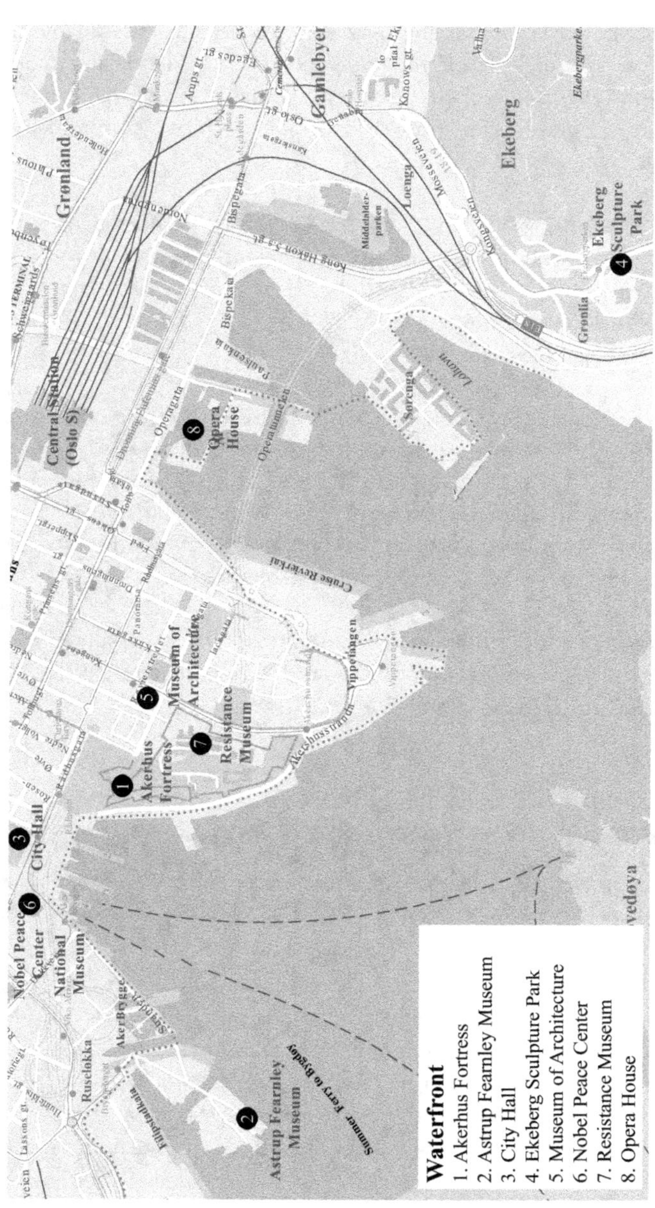
Gamlebyen
Ekeberg
Ekeberg
Ekeberg Sculpture Park
Gronland
Central Station (Oslo S)
Opera House
8
Museum of Architecture
5
Resistance Museum
7
Akerhus Fortress
1
City Hall
3
Nobel Peace Center
6
National Museum
Astrup Fearnley Museum
2
Summer Ferry to Bygdoy
Cruise Revterkai

Waterfront
1. Akerhus Fortress
2. Astrup Fearnley Museum
3. City Hall
4. Ekeberg Sculpture Park
5. Museum of Architecture
6. Nobel Peace Center
7. Resistance Museum
8. Opera House

Nobel Peace Prize

The Nobel Peace prize is awarded every November at City Hall in Oslo. All other Nobel prizes are awarded in Stockholm, Sweden. The award recognizes those who have done "the most or the best work for fraternity between nations, for the abolition or reduction of standing armies, and for the holding and promotion of peace congresses." Some notable (and controversial) winners have been:

Theodore Roosevelt (1906)
Martin Luther King, Jr. (1964)
Henry Kissinger (1973)
Mother Teresa (1979)
Mikhail Gorbachev (1990)
Nelson Mandela (1993)
Kofi Annan (2001)
Jimmy Carter (2002)
Al Gore (2007)
Barack Obama (2009)

**Astrup Fearnley Museum of Modern Art
(Astrup Fearnley Museet)**

This private collection of contemporary art has moved to a new location on the water. The museum has a collection of Norwegian and international art, with works by Francis Bacon, Damien Hirst, and Cindy Sherman. The highlight here is the lovely waterfront sculpture garden.

Info: 2 Strandpromenaden. Tel. 22 93 60 60. Closed Mon. Open Tue-Fri noon-5pm (Thu until 7pm), Sat and Sun 11am-5pm. Admission: NOK130. Under 18 free. www.afmuseet.no.

**Norwegian Resistance Museum
(Norges Hjemmefrontmuseum)**

A must for history lovers, Norway's Resistance Museum (also known as the Norwegian Home Front Museum) is located at the Akershus Fortress (see next page). The building that houses the museum dates back to the 17th century and adjoins the memorial for Norwegian patriots executed during the war. The museum focuses on Norwegian resistance during the occupation of Norway by Nazi Germany from 1940 to 1945. The collection displays photos, documents, posters, newspapers, and recordings.

Info: Akershus Fortress. Tel. 23 09 32 80. Open Sep-Apr daily 10am-4pm. Open May-Aug daily 10am-5pm. Admission: NOK60. www.forsvaretsmuseer.no/nor/Hjemmefrontmuseet.

Finding Your Way

Finding an Address
Street numbers begin on the south end of streets running north-south and on the east end of streets running east-west.
Odd numbers are on one side of the street, and even numbers on the other. In larger buildings, different businesses are designated with a letter added to the address.

Get a Free Street Map!
You can get a free detailed map of Oslo at the tourist office. You can buy a pocket-size map (with a helpful street index) at most newsstands in the city.

Akershus Fortress
(Akershus festning)

Construction of Akershus Castle and Fortress began in 1299 under King Håkon V. The medieval castle, which was completed in the 1300s, had a strategic location and withstood a number of sieges throughout the ages. King Christian IV (1588-1648) converted the structure into a Renaissances castle and royal residence. The fortress is a popular venue for concerts. One of the museums here is the Norwegian Resistance Museum (above).

Info: Akershus Castle. Tel. 23 09 39 17. Open daily 6am-9pm. Admission: Free. www.akershusfesting.no.

National Museum of Architecture
(Nasjonalmuseet-Arkitektur)

If you're looking for a place to house a museum of architecture, this building would be the choice. Formerly the Norwegian Central Bank, the building was designed in the early 1800s, and houses an extensive collection of plans and models of both classical and modern Norwegian architecture.

Info: 3 Bankplassen. Tel. 21 98 20 00. Closed Mon. Open Tue, Wed and Fri 11am-5pm, Thu 11am-7pm, Sat and Sun noon-5pm. Admission: NOK 50. Free entry on Thu. 18 and under free. www. nasjonalmuseet.no. *In 2021, the National Museum of Architecture will move to the National Museum (see p. 33).*

Opera House
(Operahuset)

The striking building that is the home of the Norwegian National Opera and Ballet sits prominently on the waterfront. It opened in 2008, and was instrumental in the revival of the harbor. The building is covered with marble from Carrara, Italy, and white granite. In contrast to the stark exterior, the interior is covered in oak. The roof of the building angles to ground level (as if rising from the water), creating a large plaza that invites visitors to walk up to the top and enjoy panoramic views of the city. From the roof, you can see the islands of the Oslofjord and the Holmenkollen Ski Jump. The opera house proudly states in its promotional materials, "In Norway, climbing mountains feels like the most natural thing to do — so why shouldn't this also apply to buildings?"

Info: 1 Kirsten Flagstads plass. Tel. 21 42 21 21. For events, check out www.operaen.no. Guided tours in English (50 minutes) Mon-Fri and Sun at 1pm, Sat at noon. NOK 120.

**Ekeberg Sculpture Park
(Ekebergparken)**

Not as popular, or conveniently located, as the sculpture garden in Frogner Park, this park offers excellent views of the city and the fjord. Among the many interesting sculptures here is Salvador Dali's *Venus de Milo aux Tiroirs*. You'll see people here reenacting Edvard Munch's famous painting *The Scream*, as this is where he is said to have been inspired to paint it.

Info: 23 Kongsvelen. Tel. 21 42 19 19. Park is always open. Admission: Free. Guided tours can be booked at www.ekebergparken.no.

Restaurants: Waterfront

Lofoten Fiskerestaurant
This elegant and award-winning restaurant is located at the end of Aker Brygge. As its name suggests, this seafood restaurant offers excellent international and Norwegian cuisine, and a stunning view of the Oslofjord. It's known for its salmon dishes. Large outdoor dining area in summer.

Info: 75 Stranden. Tel. 22 83 08 08. Open daily for lunch and dinner. www.lofotenfiskerestaurant.no. Very Expensive.

Rorbua
Decorated like a *rorbu* (fisherman's house), this bar and restaurant serves authentic Norwegian dishes, including cod, reindeer (the specialty here), and whale meat. You can even order a seagull egg! The Norwegian plate usually includes smoked whale, elk sausage, reindeer heart, moose sausage, and salmon. The bar has a large selection of beers by the bottle. In summer, there's an outdoor patio.

Info: 71 Stranden. Tel. 22 83 64 84. Open daily for lunch and dinner. www.rorbua.no. Moderate-Expensive.

Bølgen & Moi Tjuvholmen

Overlooking the docks in Akker Brygge, this location (of a Norwegian chain of restaurants) offers waterfront dining. Fish soup, burgers, pasta dishes, and salads.

Info: 5 Tjuvholmen allé. Tel. 22 44 10 20. Open Mon-Fri 11am-11pm, Sat noon-11pm, Sun 2pm-9pm. www.bolgenogmoi.no. Moderate-Expensive.

Lektern

Originally a boat, Lektern is one of the largest outdoor restaurants in Oslo. There's an immense bar, which is the perfect place to have a drink on a sunny summer day. The food is standard fare, including fish and chips, burgers, fries, fish soup, and mussels. Its unique setting and huge bar attract lots of tourists. In the evening, there's a DJ. To eat or drink here, get the number on the plaque on your table, go to the bar to order, and your order will be brought to you. See photo below.

Info: 3 Stranden. Tel. 47 21 52 32 31. Open daily in summer. www.lektern.no. Moderate.

Bygdøy

- Fram
- Kon-Tiki
- Holocaust Center
- Maritime Museum
- Museum of Cultural History (Folk Museum)
- Viking Ship Museum

To reach the museums on the Bygdøy peninsula, you can take bus #30 from Jernbanetorget (the square outside of Oslo Central Station).

From April to October, you can also take the ferry from Pier 3 near City Hall. It takes 10-15 minutes. The first stop is for the Viking Ship Museum and Museum of Cultural History. The second stop is for the Norwegian Maritime Museum, Fram, and Kon-Tiki. The Norwegian Holocaust Center is also on the peninsula. Round-trip NOK75.

**Viking Ship Museum
(Vikingskipshuset)**

The Viking Ship Museum, located on the Bygdøy peninsula, is the permanent home to three ships. The vessels date back to the 9th century, were discovered between 1867 and 1903, and are named after the places where they were discovered.

How did these huge ships survive all these years? Viking chieftains were buried in them, and to protect the fallen leaders in the afterlife, the ships were buried under mounds of clay. This protected the

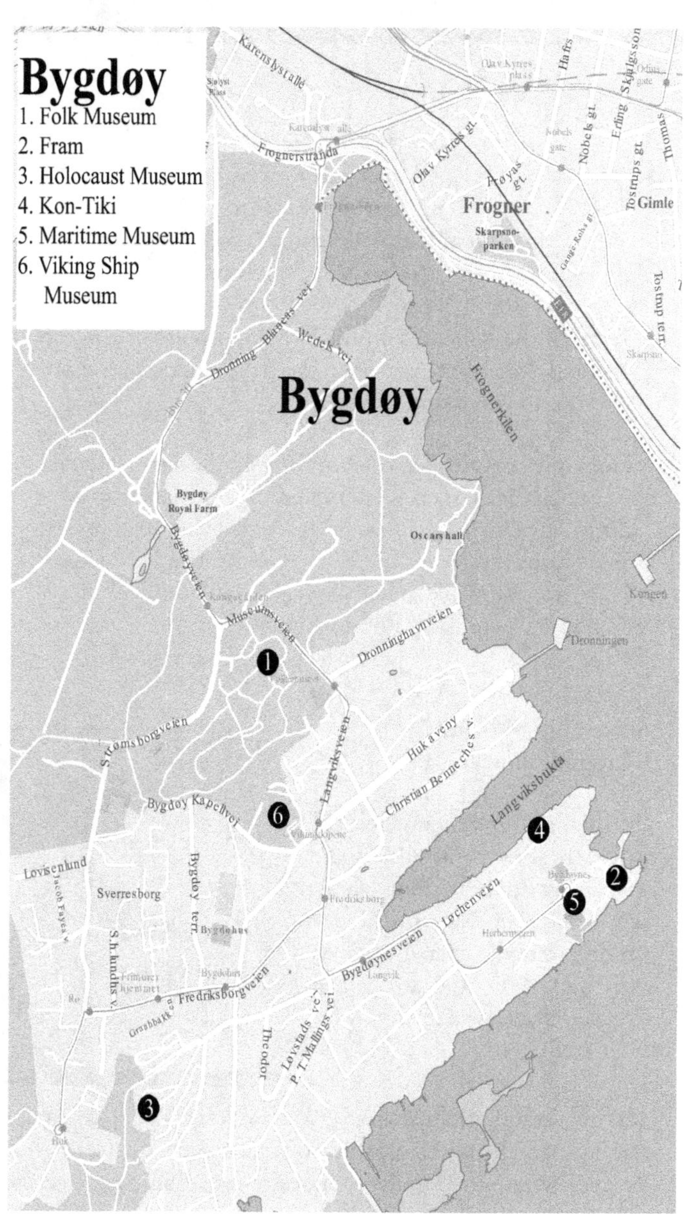

Bygdøy
1. Folk Museum
2. Fram
3. Holocaust Museum
4. Kon-Tiki
5. Maritime Museum
6. Viking Ship
   Museum
Bygdøy
Frogner

wood from decay. Chieftains were buried with their possessions so that they'd be available in the afterlife, and many of these artifacts are also on display at the museum.

The *Gokstad* dates back to a time when the Vikings of Norway were pillaging throughout Europe. The *Oseberg* has elaborate and ornate carvings, including dragon carvings and a snake's head. It's believed that this ship served as a ceremonial ship. More than 90% of this reconstructed vessel contains its original wood. The smallest (and most damaged) ship is the *Tune*.

The film *The Vikings Alive* is screened throughout the day on the ceilings and walls inside the museum. You'll also find small boats, household goods, tools, textiles, and a wooden horse cart that features carved scenes of old Viking tales.

Info: 35 Huk Aveny. Tel. 22 85 19 00. Open daily Oct-Apr 10am-4pm, May-Sep 9am-6pm. Admission: NOK120. Students and seniors NOK90. Under 18 free. www.khm.uio.no.

You can visit this museum and the Historical Museum (see page 41) for the price of one admission within 48 hours.

Norwegian Museum of Cultural History (Norsk Folkemuseum)

The Norwegian Folk Museum is a museum of cultural history with an extensive collection of artifacts from all over the country. The open-air museum (one of the largest in the world) displays 160 historic buildings relocated from Norway's towns and rural areas, dating back to the 1200s, and include churches, barns, stables, stores, and homes.

It's located on the Bygdøy peninsula near the Viking Ship Museum (see above). There's live folk music and guides in colorful, traditional folk dress. In summer, the museum offers freshly-baked *lefse*, horse and carriage rides, a petting zoo, and guided tours.

Info: 10 Museumvelen. Tel. 22 12 37 00. Open Jan-Apr and Oct-Dec 11am-4pm, May-Sep 10am-5pm. Admission: NOK160, ages 6-15 NOK40, under 6 free. norskfolkemuseum.no.

Kon-Tiki

In 1947, Thor Heyerdahl crossed the Pacific Ocean on the primitive raft Kon-Tiki. He captured his expedition on film, and was awarded the Academy Award for best documentary in 1951. He later completed similar achievements with the reed boats Ra, Ra II, and Tigris. Heyerdahl was also responsible for important excavations on Easter Island and the Galapagos Islands. This museum features objects from his famous expeditions, the Kon-Tiki raft, and the papyrus boat Ra II. Heyerdahl was a champion of the environment and world peace, and these themes run throughout this museum.

Info: 36 Bygdøynesveien. Tel. 23 08 67 67. Open daily 10am-5pm (until 4pm Nov-Feb), 9:30am-6pm (Jun-Aug). Admission: NOK120. NOK50 ages 6-15. www.kon-tiki.no.

Fram - The Polar Exploration Musem (Frammuseet)

Fram is the strongest wooden ship ever built, and holds records for sailing farthest north and south. Your visit begins with a 10-minute film giving you an introduction to polar expeditions. The museum houses the first ship to travel through the Northwest Passage.

You can go on board the ship and see how the crew (and their canines) managed to survive in the brutal Arctic and the Antarctic. Interactive exhibits include *Trapped in Ice* (a polar expedition simulator), and the stunning *Northern Lights Experience*.

Info: 26 Bygdøynesveien. Tel: 23 28 29 50. Open daily Jan-Apr and Oct-Dec 10am-5pm. May-Sep 10am-6pm. Jun-Aug 9am-6pm. Admission: NOK120 (students NOK50). www.frammuseum.no.

Holocaust Center
(Holocaustsenteret)

The Center for Studies of Holocaust and Religious Minorities (HL Center) is housed in the Villa Grande on the Bygdøy peninsula.

This high-tech center presents exhibits on the rise of anti-Semitism, the Holocaust, and racism in the world today. Films, photographs, and recordings document the mass murder and persecution of Jews and other minorities by the Nazis. Guided tours (in Norwegian and English) on Saturdays and Sundays.

Info: 56 Huk aveny. Tel. 22 84 21 00. Open mid-Sep to Mid-May 10am-4pm (mid-May to mid-Sep until 6pm). Admission: NOK70. www.hlsenteret.no.

Norwegian Maritime Museum
(Norsk Maritimt Museum)

Next door to the Fram Museum, explore more than 2,000 years of Norwegian maritime history and culture, beginning with the Viking age, at this museum with a view of the Oslofjord. The collection includes ancient boats, ship plans, photos, and a large collection of paintings from the 19th and 20th centuries. Among the highlights is the 2,200-year-old *Stokkebåten*, a canoe that is believed to be the oldest boat in Norway. Kids can operate remote-controlled boat models in the exhibition's pool, and construct their own model boat at The Children's Boat Workshop. The workshop is open every Sunday afternoon.

There's also a 20-minute movie (spread across five screens) which takes you on a journey along Norway's coast. It's shown every 30 minutes in the museum's movie theater.

Info: 37 Bygdøynesvelen. Tel. 22 12 37 00. Open Oct-Apr 11am-4pm, May-Sep 10am-5pm. Admission: NOK120, NOK50 ages 6-15, under 6 free. www.marmuseum.no.

Restaurants: Bygdøy

Kafé Villa Grande

The café in the Villa Grande (which houses the Holocaust Center) serves international and Norwegian dishes, salads, sandwiches, and pastries. There's also a lovely garden where you can dine. Convenient when visiting the museums on the peninsula.

Info: 56 Huk aveny. Tel. 67 10 99 70. Open Tue-Sun 11am-4pm. Closed Mon. www.hlsenteret.no. Moderate.

Café hjemme hos svigers

If you're looking for a lunch spot near the Viking, Fram, and Maritime museums, this is a good choice. It's both a café and an antique shop and is located in the old post office on the Bygdøy peninsula. Everything (including tables, chairs, and plates) is for sale. The menu includes burgers, sandwiches, salads, and soups. Most dishes can be served gluten- and lactose-free. An interesting place to eat.

Info: 16 Fredriksborgveien. Tel. 22 55 62 26. Open Tue-Sun 11am-6pm. Closed Mon. cafehjemmehossvigers.no. Moderate.

City Center

* Cathedral
* National Gallery
* National Museum of Architecture
* Parliament
* Royal Palace

Oslo Central Station
(Oslo S)

Oslo Central Station (also called Oslo S) is the main transportation hub in Oslo. The train station, the largest in Norway, is the end of the Drammen, Gardermoen, Gjøvik, Hoved, and Østfold lines, and has local, regional, and express train services. The station is made up of two buildings, the original Oslo East building and the newer main building. Each building is home to large shopping centers. It's the cleanest train station we've ever seen!

The square in front of the station is Jernbanetorget. Trams and some city buses stop here. You can connect to all six subway lines at the Jernbanetorget subway station. The bus terminal is located near the station at the Oslo Bus Terminal.

National Museum
(Nasjonalmuseet)

The new National Museum, centrally located between City Hall and Aker Brygge, is scheduled to open in 2021. It will combine the National Gallery, Museum of Contemporary Art, the National Museum of Architecture, and the Museum of Decorative Arts and Design (Kunstindustrimuseet). (The Museum of Contemporary Art, Museum of Decorative Arts and Design, and National Gallery are currently closed until the opening of the new National Museum). It will be the largest art museum in Scandinavia.

"Tiger City"

When you arrive in Oslo at Central Station, you'll notice a large bronze statue of a tiger. Oslo is called "The Tiger City." There are many explanations for the nickname. It was likely first used by a Norwegian poet in 1870, describing a fight between a tiger and a horse; the tiger represented the dangerous city, and the horse the safe countryside.

Some say that the nickname came from folks from the countryside moving to "The Tiger."

The nickname also has a dark side. Oslo, or Christiania as it was called then, went under the name "tiggerstaden" (city of beggars) by Danes and people from more affluent western parts of the country due to the city's high level of poverty.

Over the years, the nickname has almost achieved official status. Oslo's 1000-year anniversary was celebrated with sculptures of tigers around city hall.

Oslo's Main Street

Karl Johans Gate is Oslo's main street. This pedestrian boulevard runs from the Central Station through the center of town to the stately Royal Palace. It's lined with restaurants, hotels, parks, and landmarks. Along the boulevard, you'll find the Cathedral and Parliament. Also here is the bustling Stortorvet (the city's grand plaza). The statue on the grand plaza is King Christian IV who, when ruler of Denmark and Norway, established Oslo.

The grand plaza is also the sight of a large produce and flower market.

National Gallery
(Nasjonalgalleriet)

Founded in 1837, the National Gallery houses Norway's largest public collection of paintings, drawings, and sculptures.

The Scream, *Madonna*, *The Sick Child*, and *The Dance of Life* are some of the highlights of the museum's collection of works by Edvard Munch. Works by other leading Norwegian artists, such as J.C. Dahl and Thomas Fearnley, are also highlighted.

The collection also features works by such notables as Manet, Cézanne, Monet, and van Gogh.

Especially popular for kids is The Fairy Tale Room with art depicting trolls and other fairy tale creatures. In The Drawing Room you can practice your sketching skills while drawing Gustav Vigeland's 1907 sculpture *Mother and Child*.

If you're hungry after viewing all that art, you can grab a bite to eat at The French Salon. This elegant café, located in the museum, was designed in 1924 to house sculptures gifted from France.

Info: 13 Universitetsgata. Tel. 21 98 20 00. Closed Mon. Open 11am-6pm (Sat and Sun until 5pm). Admission: NOK100. Free entry on Thu. 18 and under free. English audio guide NOK50. www.nasjonalmuseet.no. *The National Gallery closed in January 2019 and will reopen in the new National Museum in 2021.*

Grand Cafe

Oslo's main boulevard, Karl Johans Gate, is home to the Grand Café. This luxurious cafe opened in 1874. Henrik Ibsen, Norway's famous writer, would frequently eat his lunch here. Norway's most famous painter, Edvard Munch, offered to barter a painting in exchange for 100 dinners. The wine cellar holds over 16,000 bottles representing more than 1,500 wines from all around the world.

Info: 31 Karls Johans Gate. Tel. 98 18 20 00. Open Mon-Fri 11am-11pm, Sat noon-11pm, Sun noon-9pm. Wine cellar opens Tue-Fri at 4pm, Sat at 2pm. Wine cellar is closed Sun and Mon. www. grandcafeoslo.no.

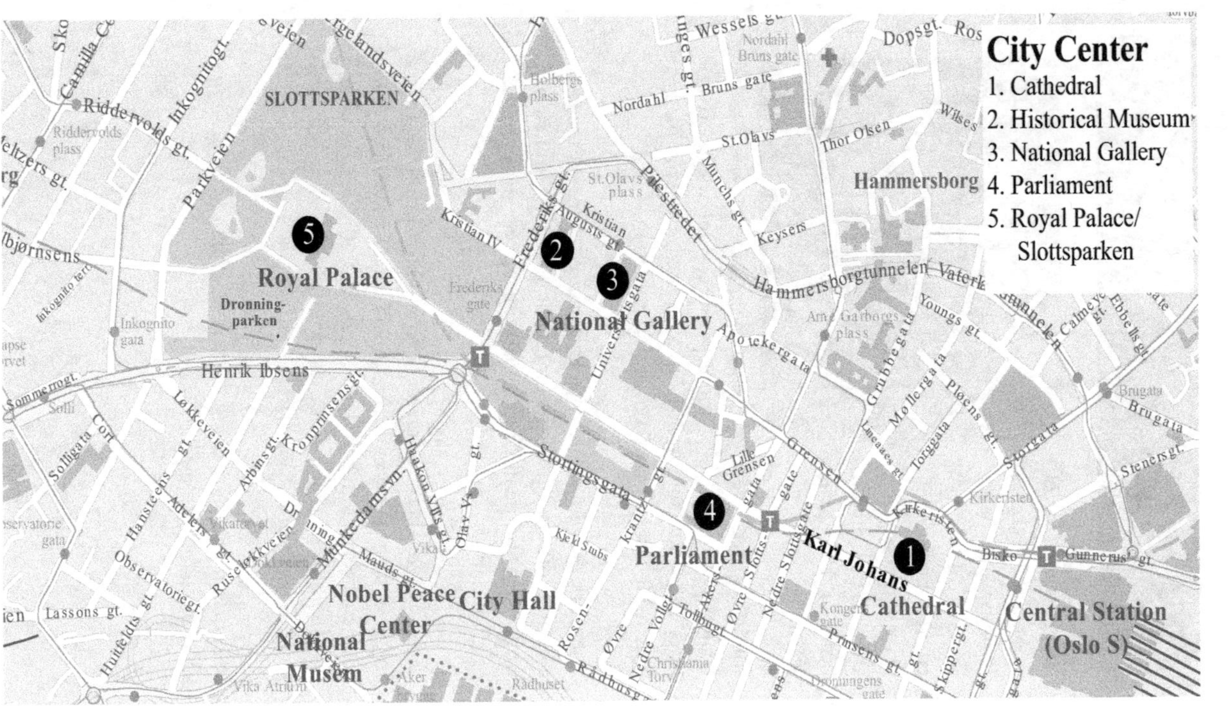
City Center
1. Cathedral
2. Historical Museum
3. National Gallery
4. Parliament
5. Royal Palace/
Slottsparken
SLOTTSPARKEN
Royal Palace
Dronning-parken
National Gallery
Karl Johans
Cathedral
Parliament
Central Station (Oslo S)
Nobel Peace City Hall
National Center Museum
Henrik Ibsens
Hammersborg
Hammersborgtunnelen
Stortingsgata
Universitets gata
Apotekergata
Kristian IV
Frederiks gate
Kristian Augusts gt.
Pilestredet
St.Olavs plass
Munchs gt.
Keysers
St.Olavs
Thor Olsen
Wilses
Nordahl Bruns gate
Nordahl
Bruns gate
Wessels gt.
Inges gt.
Holbergs plass
Dopsgt.
Ros
Parkveien
Inkognitogt.
Riddervolds gt.
Riddervolds plass
Camilla C.
Meltzers gt.
Ulbjørnsens
Inkognito terr.
Inkognito gata
Sommerogt.
Solli
Løkkeveien
Kronprinsens gt.
Arbinsgt.
Haakon VII's gt.
Drammensvn.
Munkedamsvn.
Olav V gt.
Vika
Mauds gt.
Kjeld Stubs
Kranz
Lille Grensen
Grensen
Øvre Slottsgate
Nedre Slottsgate
Akersgata
Øvre Voll gt.
Nedre Voll gt.
Tollbugt.
Kongens gate
Prinsens gt.
Dronningens gate
Skippergt.
Bisko
Gunnerus gt.
Kirkeristen
Youngs gt.
Grubbegata
Møllergata
Pløens gt.
Linneaes gt.
Torggata
Storgata
Brugata
Stenersgt.
Calmeyer gt.
Ebbells gt.
Vaterland
Arne Garborgs plass
Solligata
Cort
Hansteens gt.
Adelers gt.
Ruseløkkveien
Observatoriegt.
Lassons gt.
Huitfeldts
Observatorie gata
Aker
Vika Atrium
Rådhuset
Rosen-
Christiania Torv

Norway's Most Famous Work of Art

The Scream (_Skrik_) is one of the most famous works of art in the world. It was created by Norwegian Expressionist artist Edvard Munch between 1893 and 1910.

Munch created several versions in various media. The National Gallery is home to this famous painting. One version (pastel from 1895) was sold in 2012 to a private buyer who paid the fourth-highest price for a painting at auction.

The work shows a figure with an agonized expression against a tumultuous orange sky in a moment of anguish and despair, while the other people in the painting appear to be unaware of his situation.

The Scream has been the target of several high-profile art thefts. In 1994, the version in the National Gallery was stolen. It was recovered several months later. In 2004, both _The Scream_ and _Madonna_ were stolen from the Munch Museum, but both were recovered two years later.

The National Gallery closed in January 2019 and will reopen in the new National Museum in 2021.

Oslo Cathedral
(Oslo Domkirke)

Consecrated in 1697, the interior of Oslo's cathedral was restored in 1950 to its original baroque style. The altar, pulpit, and carved organ are all original. The ceiling murals were painted between 1936 and 1950. It's used for public events by the Royal Family and the government, and is a frequent venue for concerts.

An interesting feature here are the bazaar halls (**Basarhallene**) located behind the cathedral and built in the 19th century. The arcaded halls are now home to cafes, restaurants, boutiques, and antique stores. They were originally used as butcher shops.

Info: 11 Karl Johans gate. Tel. 23 62 90 10. Open daily 10am-4pm. Admission: Free. www.kirken.no.

Norwegian Parliament
(Stortinget)

Built in the 19th century, Norway's Parliament faces the Royal Palace. An interesting feature is that the chambers have windows that overlook the square to represent transparency and public participation in government. English tours are available on most Saturday mornings (you can't visit alone). Since this is a government building, you should check the website beforehand to make sure that the tours are operating. Eidsvolle plass is the popular and fountain-filled square in front of Parliament.

Info: 23 Karl Johans gate. Tel. 23 31 50 50. www.stortinget.no.

**Royal Palace
(Det kongelige slott)**

The Royal Palace is situated at the end of Oslo's main thorough-fare, Karl Johans gate. The foundation stone was laid in 1825. The palace is the official residence of the King and Queen, and is where the King presides over the Council of State, grants audiences, and holds official dinners. Foreign heads of state who visit Oslo stay here.

The changing of the guard takes place daily at 1:30pm. The guardhouse here is said to be the oldest building in Norway. You can take a one-hour guided tours (in English) during the summer, but you must book in advance.

Info: 1 Slottesplatten. Tel. 22 04 87 00. www.kongehuset.no and royalcourt.no.

Slottsparken

Although Frogner Park get most of the attention, this lovely park around the Royal Palace should not be missed. Three ponds, flowering meadows in summer, and a peaceful atmosphere make this a pleasant place to stroll.

Queen Sonja Art Stable

The former royal stables, built in the 19th century, have been converted to an art space featuring changing exhibits. Opened on the 80th birthday of Queen Sonja, the permanent collection features photographs of the royal family.

Info: Slottsparken (see above). Entrance on Parkveien. Tel. 22 04 87 00. Open 11am-5pm Thu-Sun. Admission: NOK100. www.royalcourt.no.

Historical Museum
(Kulturhistorisk Museum)

This museum is home to Norway's largest cultural and historic collections. Viking treasures, the country's oldest skull, Egyptian mummies, and articles from the Artic expeditions are all found in this beautiful Art-Nouveau (Jugend) building.

Info: 2 Frederiks gate. Tel 22 85 19 00. Open Oct-Apr Tue-Sun 11am-4pm. May-Sep 10am-5pm. Closed Mon. Admission: NOK120. Students and seniors NOK90. Under 18 free. www.khm.uio.no.

You can visit this museum and the Viking Museum (see pages 27-28) for the price of one admission within 48 hours.

Restaurants: City Center

Den Glade Gris

"The Happy Pig" gastropub specializes in pork-based dishes, and the house specialty is grilled pork knuckle. Its large menu features everything from fish and chips to reindeer sausage (which we loved!). The pub serves nearly 30 different bottled beers and eight beers on tap from Norwegian breweries. Friendly service and an outdoor patio in good weather.

Info: 33 St. Olavsgate (near both the large Radisson Blue and Thon Hotels). Tel. 22.11.17.10. Open Mon-Fri 11am-11pm, Sat noon-11pm, and Sun 4pm-11pm. www.dengladgris.no.

Illegal Burgers

Char-grilled burgers and fat fries are served at this popular burger joint located a few blocks from the Oslo Cathedral.

Info: 23 Møllergata. Tel. 22.20.33.02. Open Mon-Thu 11am-11pm, Fri and Sat 2pm-1am, Sun 2pm-11pm. Inexpensive.

Justisen

This lovely restaurant and bar (with wood-paneled rooms) dates back to 1928 and is located a few blocks from the Oslo Cathedral. The menu eclectic features Norwegian and international specialties. An added bonus is the fun beer garden.

Info: 15 Møllergata. Tel. 22.42.24.72. Open Wed-Sat 4pm-3am. Closed Sun-Tue. www.justisen.no. Moderate-Expensive.

West

- City Museum
- Frogner Park
- Vigeland Sculpture Park

Frogner Park and the Vigeland Sculpture Park

Frogner Park is the largest park in central Oslo and has Norway's biggest collection of plants (14,000) of 150 different species.

Inside the park you'll find the **Vigeland Sculpture Park**, one of Oslo's most popular attractions. This is a *must* for any visit to Oslo!

The sculpture park has more than 200 (mostly nude) sculptures in bronze, granite, and wrought iron by Gustav Vigeland (1869–1943). Vigeland also designed the park.

Wandering this park is truly an incredible experience. We've never been to such a thought-provoking park!

Info: The park is open year round and is free.

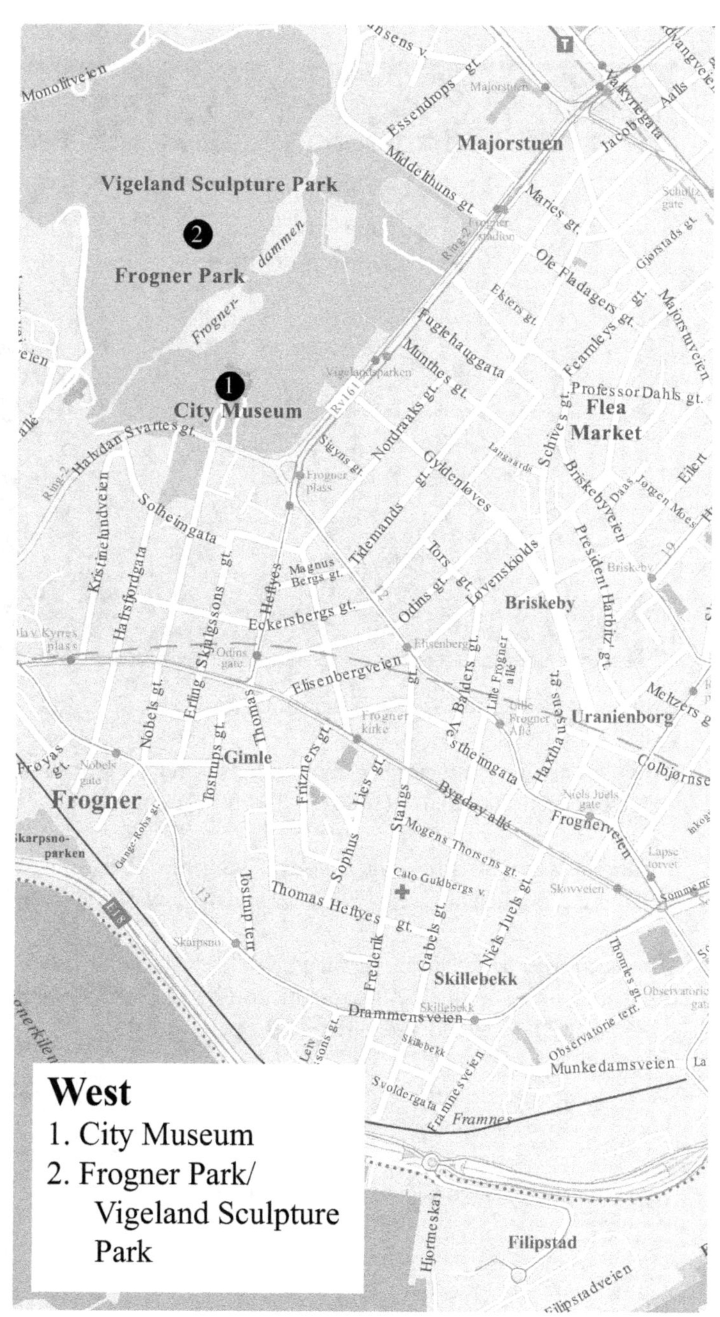

West

1. City Museum
2. Frogner Park/
   Vigeland Sculpture
   Park

Don't miss *The Angry Boy* (*Sinnataggen*) whose hand (and another body part) is a different color from so many touching it because it will supposedly bring you good luck. The highlight is *The Monolith* (*Monolitten*) featuring 121 figures writhing on top of one another. (pictured on the front of this book).

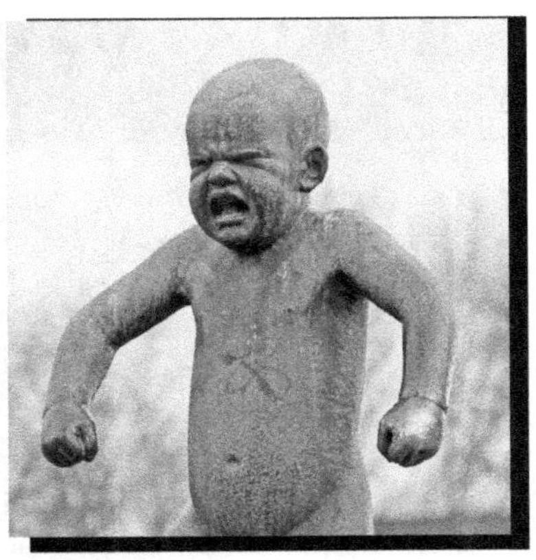

For more information on the park and its creator Gutav Vigeland, see the next page.

Also here is the **City Museum (Bymuseet)**, located in an 18th-century manor, tracking the history of Oslo through its large collection of photographs and paintings.

Info: Southern portion of Frogner Park. 67 Frognerveien. Tel. 23 28 41 70. Closed Mon. Open Tue-Sun 11am-4pm. Admission: NOK90. Under 18 free. Free first Sat of every month. English audio guide available. www.oslomuseum.no.

Vestkanttorget Flea Market

Some Norwegian's junk might just be your favorite souvenir. Dig through the stuff every Saturday morning. The market is located one block east of Frogner Park at the square on Professor Dahls gate. Closed winter.

Gustav Vigeland

Vigeland, Norway's most famous sculptor, designed Frogner Park, and his works are featured in the park's Vigeland Sculpture Park. He also designed the Nobel Peace Prize medal.

Vigeland spent the 1890s outside of Norway. He traveled and studied in Denmark, Germany, France, and Italy. In Paris he frequented Auguste Rodin's workshop. He held his first exhibitions in Norway in 1894 and 1896, which received critical praise.

When Norway became independent from Sweden in 1905, Vigeland, who was considered the country's most talented sculptor, received government commissions for statues and busts celebrating famous Norwegians. In 1921, he was given a state-subsidized studio and apartment. In exchange, he promised to donate all of his works to the state.

Vigeland was a troubled man said to have Nazi, or at least fascist, sympathies. Keep this in mind when you stroll Frogner Park. You'll see a woman who stands back to back with her lover, an elderly couple hugging, an angry child, and human forms climbing to the sky.

Vigeland's sculpture garden is one of the largest sculpture parks in the world, and the largest by a single artist. It's truly an interesting experience and Frogner Park is one of the loveliest city parks in the world.

Travel Stuff

Nomaden

If this guide isn't enough for your trip, you'll find maps, travel guides, and travel literature at this travel bookstore. They also sell backpacking supplies, clothing, hats, and travel accessories (like electric converters). Norwegians are huge travelers and this is Norway's largest travel store.

Info: 4 Uranienborgveien. Tel. 23.13.14.15. Open Mon-Fri 10am-6pm, Sat until 5pm. Open Mon-Fri 10am-6pm, Sat 10am-5pm. Closed Sun. www.nomaden.no.

Restaurants: West

Rust

This popular Italian restaurant is located near the Royal Palace. You'll find mostly locals at this small trattoria. The menu includes such Italian favorites as cannelloni and lasagne. There's also a selection of small plates. The wine list features wines from many of Italy's wine regions. In nice weather, you can dine outdoors. The menu is in Italian and Norwegian, but you'll be able to figure it out with the help of your server.

Info: 22 Hegdehaugsveien (off of Parkveien). Tel. 94 01 57 50. Open Mon-Sat noon-11pm, Sun noon-7pm. www.rustoslo.com. Moderate-Expensive.

Champagneria

Bubbly anyone? French champagne, Italian *prosecco*, and Spanish *cava* are served by the bottle and glass at this two-story bar. You can down your bubbly with a selection of *tapas*. Open late.

Info: 2 Frognerveien. Tel. 21 08 09 09. Open Mon-Wed 4pm-1am. Thu-Fri until 3am. Sat 1pm-3am. Sun 4pm-11pm. www.champagneria.com. Moderate-Expensive.

Apent Bakeri

This bakery is located in the neighborhood behind Slottsparken (the park sourrounding the Royal Palace). It serves fresh croissants, substantial sandwiches, excellent pastries, and delicious coffee and tea. Lovely outdoor seating on a quite street adds to the experience.

Info: 1 Inkognito Terrasse (off of Colbjørnsens gate). Tel. 92 04 65 43. Open Mon-Fri 7:30am-5pm, Sat 8am-4pm, Sun 9am-4pm. www.apentbakeri.no. Moderate.

Forest & Brown

Attractive English pub and restaurant in the Frogner area. Large selection of beer by the bottle and on tap. This neighborhood hangout serves burgers, salads, nachos, and pasta dishes.

Info: 31 Niels Juels gate (off of Bygdøy Allé). Tel. 22 55 26 80. Open Mon-Thu 11am-1am, Fri 11am-2:30am, Sat noon-2:30am, and Sun noon-1am. www.forestandbrown.no. Moderate-Expensive.

East/Grünerløkka/Grønland

* Mathallen/Food Hall
* Munch Museum
* University Botanical Gardens/Natural
History Museum

**Munch Museum
(Munchmuseet)**

Edvard Munch is Norway's most famous artist, and is considered a pioneer in expressionism. The museum's collection was left to the city by Munch, and includes his paintings, prints, and drawings. A film on Munch's life introduces visitors to the artist. Note: The original of his most famous painting, *The Scream*, is not here. It's been temporarily replaced with *The Madonna*. The museum will move in 2020/2021 to its new site on the waterfront, next to the Oslo Opera House. Munch was quite a prolific artist: The museum's collection consists of 1,150 paintings, 17,800 graphic works, 7,700 drawings, 14 sculptures, besides numerous photographs taken by Munch himself. Guided tours in English every day in July and August at 1pm.

Info: 53 Tøyengata. Tel. 23 49 35 00. Open daily 10am-4pm (until 5pm in summer). Admission: NOK 120. Under 18 free. www.munchmuseet.no.

**University Botanical Garden/Natural History Museum
(Universitetets Botaniske hage/Naturhistorisk museum)**

This lovely, large botanical garden plants from throughout Norway. A section has a Viking theme, and focuses on natural resources during the Viking age. The Natural History Museum here is known for housing the world's oldest primate skeleton. They've

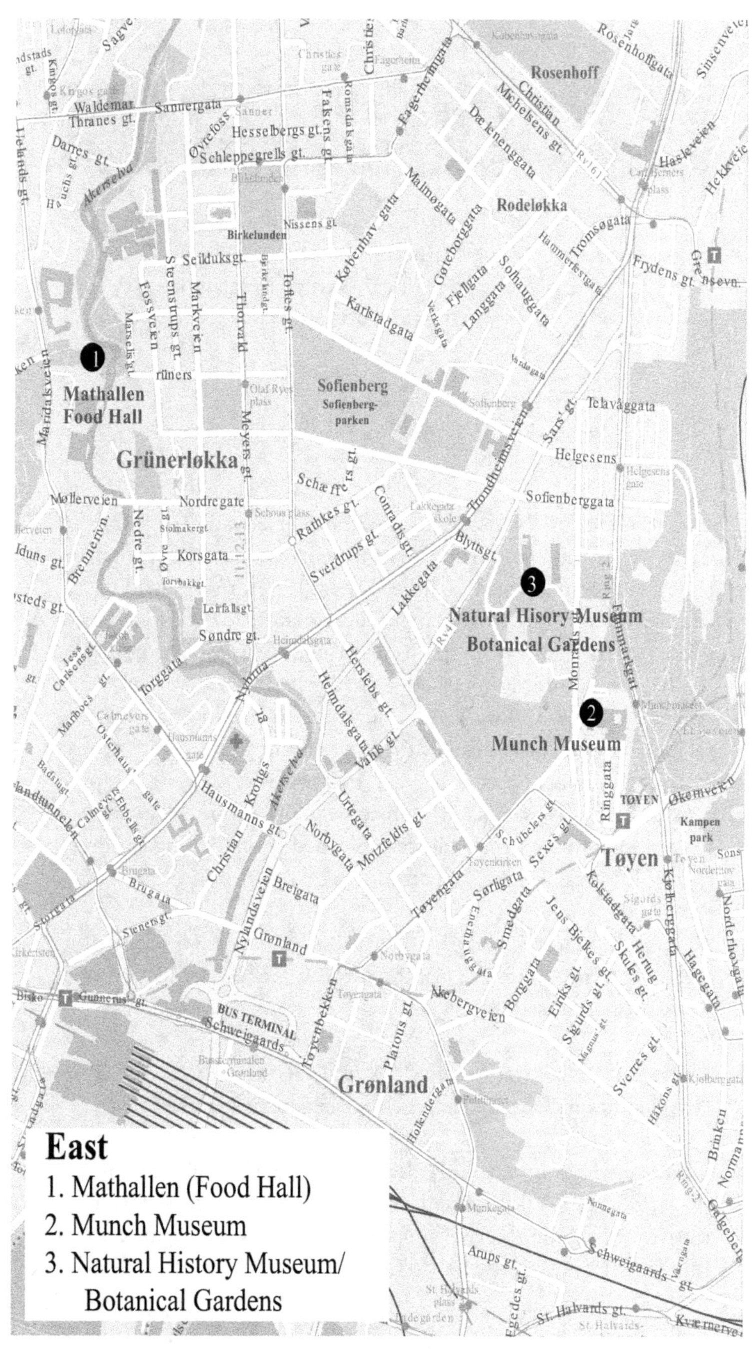

East

1. Mathallen (Food Hall)
2. Munch Museum
3. Natural History Museum/
   Botanical Gardens

named the skeleton "Ida", and scientists have dated her to 47.8 million years.

Info: 1 Sars' gate. Tel. 22 85 16 30 (botanical garden). Museum open Tue-Fri 11am-4pm, Sat and Sun 10am-5pm. Admission: NOK50. Botanical garden open daily 7am-5pm. Admission: Free (botanical garden), NOK120 (museum). www.nhm.uio.no.

Time to Climb!

Vulkan Climbing

This indoor climbing center has both climbing walls and boulder walls. Many different classes for children, adults, and the disabled.

Info: 13 Vulkan (off of Maridalsveien). Near the Marthallen (Food Hall). Tel. 22 11 28 90. Open daily. www.kolsaas.no. Admission: From NOK80.

Mathallen
(Food Hall)

Let's face it, Norway has not been known as a destination for eating. Things are changing, partly because of the influx of other ethnic groups. Oslo's wonderful indoor food market has more than 30 specialty shops, eateries, and cafés.

When you look at the diversity found here, you'll quickly realize that dining in Norway and Oslo is not what it once was. Just a few offerings here include:

Annis Pølsemakeri - sausages and cured meats
Barramon - wine bar with Spanish tapas
Bistro Budapest - Hungarian food and wine
Champagneria Bodega - wine bar with tapas
Hitchhiker - restaurant and bar serving international fare
Hopyard - bar with more than 200 types of beer and American food
Modern Greens - salad bar
Obento Box - Japanese-inspired foods
Ost & Sånt - Norwegian cheese, jam, and cured meats
Paradis Gelateria - Italian gelato
Pizzavino - pizza and wine
SebastienBruno - chocolate and candy shop
The Cupcake & Pie Co. - pies and cupcakes
Via Italia - Italian food products
Vulkan frukt og grønt - fruit, vegetables, spices, sauces, and oils
Vulkanfisk - seafood restaurant

Info: 17 Maridalsveien. Tel. 40 00 12 09. Open daily. Each eatery has its own hours. www.mathallenoslo.no.

Junk!

Marita
This is one of those places where you can spend way too much time. This charity shop is jammed with rummage. You'll find glasses, dishes, and household goods. Upstairs is filled with records, CDs, and books.

Info: 12 Gladengveien. Tel. 21 05 26 00. Open Tue and Thu noon-6pm, Sat 11am-3pm.
www.marita.no.

RESTAURANTS: EAST

This area is known for its diverse dining options. In addition to all the options offered at the Mathallen food hall (see earlier), here are just a few other dining options, from inexpensive to very expensive.

Syverkiosken

The Norwegians love *pølser* (hot dogs). You can sample the dogs at this simple eatery. Top it off with one of the many condiments offered (and make sure you try the fiery mustard). This is one of the last remaining kiosks in Oslo. It's also one of the cheapest snack options, as dogs start at NOK20.

Info: 45 Maridalsveien. Open daily.

Taco República

Norwegian tacos? This taqueria may not be exactly what you would find in Southern California, but it's worth a try. Inexpensive tacos are served in a festive space. Try the fish tacos!

Info: 30 Torgatta. Tel. 40 05 76 65. Open Tue 4pm-10pm, Wed-Thu 4pm-11pm, Fri-Sat 3pm-midnight, Sun 2pm-10pm. Closed Mon. www.tacorepublica.no. Tacos from NOK60.

Kontrast

Unlike the dining choices above, this award-winning restaurant, located in a stark, industrial space, is not for those on a budget. The dishes feature organic and locally produced ingredients. The six-course tasting menu (NOK1450) includes such innovative dishes as duck breast cured in juniper and coffee. Ten courses from NOK 1950.

Info: 15a Maridalsveien. Tel. 21 60 01 01. Reservations required. www.restaurant-kontrast.no. Very Expensive.

Villa Paradiso

Norwegians love pizza and, according to whom you ask, this noisy one is among the best places in Oslo to get your Italian fix. In good weather, you can dine outside. Interesting wine list featuring selections from throughout Italy.

Info: 8 Olaf Ryes plass. Tel. 22 35 40 60. Open daily. www.villaparadiso.no. Moderate.

Handwerk

You'll feel you're in the countryside at this peaceful cafe in the center of the Botanical Garden, where large windows provide lovely garden views. The former farm building has a pale-blue interior and is decorated with floral artwork (appropriate for the botanical surroundings). Sandwiches, soups, salads, and simple fare. Great place for a glass of wine after visiting the garden.

Info: 1 Sarsgate. Tel. 22 60 85 00. Open daily for lunch and dinner. www.handwerk.no. Moderate. Also at 15E Maridalsvn (Vulkan). Tel 22 60 85 00. Open daily

Olympen

Chandeliers, wood-panel walls, and murals from the 1920s all add to the charm of this neighborhood landmark. Norwegian and international specialties (they have steak, fish, and pork dishes) are served here, so you can start with herring, but if you're not feeling adventurous, switch to a club sandwich. Beer lovers can choose from nearly 100 beers from throughout the world.

Info: 15 Grønlandsleiret. Tel. 24 10 19 99. Open daily for lunch and dinner. www.olympen.no. Moderate-Expensive.

Bass Oslo

Norway is not known for its wine, although you will find some rhubarb and apple wines. But, this doesn't mean you can't find excellent wine lists. This wine bar and restaurant is located in the Grünerløkka neighborhood. The decor is interesting (cement walls, painted black furniture, and a plywood bar). There's a large international wine menu including many natural wines available. The small plates feature interesting combinations like fried free-range chicken with black-bean mayonnaise.

Info: 26 Thorvald Meyers gate. Tel. 48.24.14.89. Dinner only. Closed Mon. www.bassoslo.no. Moderate-Expensive.

It's Expensive!

You've most likely heard that Norway is expensive. It is! The country has one of the highest standards of living, and salaries are generous. Norwegians have benefited from vast oil reserves, with free education and health care. Food, accommodations, and transporation are all more expensive than most other European destinations. Alcoholic beverages are highly taxed, and especially expensive. A beer in a bar usually costs at least $10 US dollars.

Holmenkollen

- **Holmenkollen Ski Museum and Ski Jump**
- **Science & Technology Museum**

Holmenkollen Ski Museum and Ski Jump

Holmenkollen is the hill to the northwest of Oslo. It takes 20-30 minutes to get to the area from the center of the city. By public transportation, you must take the T-Bane (Line 1) to the Holmenkollen stop. Be warned that from the T-Bane stop, it's a 10-minute walk (uphill) to the Ski Museum.

Skiing and ski jumping are rooted in Norwegian culture. The ski museum in Holmenkollen, located underneath the famous ski jump, is the oldest of its kind in the world. The museum explores skiing from prehistoric times to today. The ski hill's use in the 1952 Winter Olympics is also explored. If you've ever wondered what it's like to ski jump, the museum has a simulator. This is a great feature for those of us (like this author) who are way too chicken to actually ski jump! After visiting the museum, take the elevator to the top. You'll have panoramic views of Oslo and the surrounding countryside.

If you're feeling adventurous, you can take the zip line down to the base. The Kollensvevet Zip Line operates from April through mid-October. Note that the line only operates on weekends during

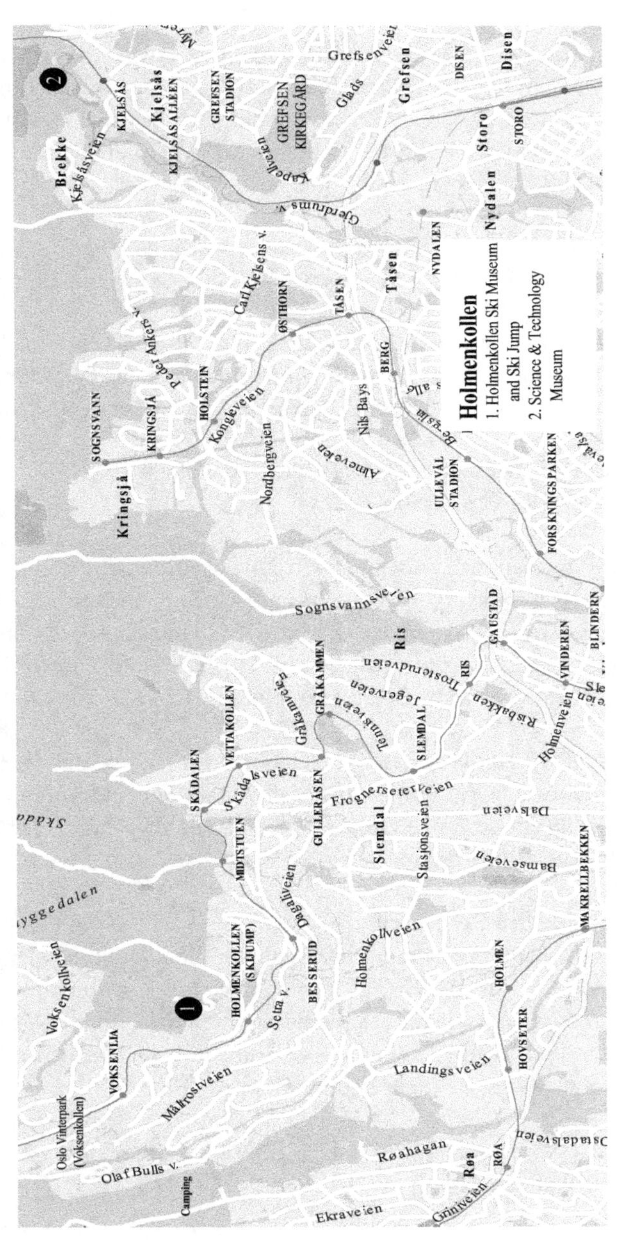
Grefsenveien
Grefsen
DISEN
Disen
Gladsveien
GREFSEN KIRKEGARD
GREFSEN STADION
Glads
Grefsen
Myrerveien
Kjelsås
KJELSÅS
KJELSÅSALLÉEN
Kjelsås
Kjelsåsveien
Nydalen
Storo
STORO
Brekke
Kjelsåsveien
Kapellveien
NYDALEN
Gjerdrums v.
Carl Kjelsens v.
Tåsen
ØSTHORN
TÅSEN
BERG
Berg s. allé
Holmenkollen
1. Holmenkollen Ski Museum and Ski Jump
2. Science & Technology Museum
Peder Ankers v.
HOLSTEN
Kongleveien
Nils Bays
Nordbergveien
Almeveien
Bergslia
ULLEVÅL STADION
FORSKNINGSPARKEN
SOGNSVANN
KRINGSJÅ
Kringsjå
Sognsvannsveien
Ris
GAUSTAD
BLINDERN
VINDEREN
RES
Trosterudveien
Risbakken
Holmenveien
Slemdalsveien
GRÅKAMMEN
Gråkamveien
VETTAKOLLEN
Tennisveien
Jegerveien
SLEMDAL
SKÅDALEN
Skådals veien
GULLERÅSEN
Frognerseterveien
Slemdal
Stasjonsveien
Dalsveien
Skådalen
MIDTSTUEN
Dagaliveien
Bamseveien
MAKRELLBEKKEN
Voksenkollveien
yggedalen
HOLMENKOLLEN (SKIJUMP)
BESSERUD
Setra v.
Holmenkollveien
HOLMEN
VOKSENLIA
Landingsveien
HOVSETER
Oslo Vinterpark (Voksenkollen)
Målrostveien
VOKSENKOLLEN
Røahagan
Røa
ROA
Ostdalsveien
Olaf Bulls v.
Camping
Ekraveien
Grinveien

these months except mid-June through August when it operates Mon-Fri 11am-6pm, Sat and Sun noon-6pm. There will likely be a line. Check ahead for reservations and opening times at www.kollensvevet.no. The cost is from NOK679 (and an additional NOK500 if you make reservations).

The Holmenkollen area is a gateway to **Nordmarka**, one of the most popular recreational areas near Oslo for skiing and hiking.

Info: 5 Kongeveien. Tel. 22 92 32 00. Museum open daily 10am-4pm (May and Sep until 5pm). Open Jun-Aug 9am-8pm. Admission: NOK 150. www.skiforeningen.no/en/holmenkollen/.

**Norwegian Museum of Science and Technology
(Norsk Teknisk Museum)**

Norway's national museum for technology, industry, and science was founded over 100 years ago. Much of the museum is designed with kids in mind, offering over 80 interactive exhibits. The National Museum of Medicine is integrated in the museum, and features historical medical exhibits.

Info: 143 Kjelsåsveien. Tel. 22 79 60 00. Open Tue-Fri 9am-4pm, Sat and Sun 11am-6pm. Open daily 11am-6pm mid-June to mid-Aug. Admission: NOK165, NOK110 children and students www.tekniskmuseum.no.

Holmenkollen Restaurant
Near the famous ski jump, this restaurant offers stunning views (especially at sunset). The rustic interior, complete with fireplace and moose heads, is especially inviting in winter. International fare is offered, with an emphasis on game dishes. It's expensive, as you're paying for the incredible view.

Info: 119 Holmenkollveien. Tel. 22 13 92 00. Closed Mon. www.holmenkollenrestaurant.no. Expensive.

Oslo Neighborhoods

Central Oslo
Karl Johans Gate, Oslo's main street, connects Central Station and the Royal Palace. Many museums (including the National Gallery), hotels, and eateries are here.

Old Town
(Gamlebyen)
This area is south of the Parliament Building (Stortinget) and Karl Johans Gate. You'll find the Norwegian Resistance Museum and the Old Town Hall here, along with plenty of restaurants.

Aker Brygge and the Waterfront
Now that the former shipbuilding yards are gone, the waterfront is an excellent place for walking, dining, and cultural attractions (including the fabulous Opera House).

West
This upscale residential area is home to some of the city's best hotels and restaurants. Frogner Park (Frognerparken) is here, where you'll find the hugely popular Vigeland Sculpture Park.

East
Some popular sights are found in this area, including the Botanic Garden, the Natural History Museum, and the popular Munch Museum.

Bygdøy
You can reach this peninsula, west of the city center, by bus or ferry (in the summer), where you'll find a cluster of museums, including the Viking Ship Museum, Norwegian Folk Museum, Fram Museum, Kon-Tiki Museum, Maritime Museum, and Holocaust Museum.

Grønland

Multicultural area where refugees from India, Pakistan, and other countries have settled. (One in three residents of Oslo was born outside the country.) Affordable dining can be found at its many ethnic restaurants.

Grünerløkka

Oslo's bohemian district is filled with bars, cafes, and restaurants. This trendy district in east Oslo was once home to mostly the working class. It's being gentrified, and many have moved in to renovate property.

Oslofjord

Take a ferry and visit the small islands in this fjord located in front of the city.

Holmenkollen

Easily reached from central Oslo, this area is in the hills northwest of the city. Popular with skiers and hikers. You can visit the Ski Museum and Ski Jump Hill here.

Marka

The forested and hilly areas surrounding Oslo, it's a sprawling recreation area with over 300 lakes, 300 miles (500km) of ski trails, hundreds of miles of hiking trails, and 24 ski jumps and alpine slopes.

Excursion to Lillehammer

Little **Lillehammer** (only 27,000 people call it home) was the site of the 1994 Winter Olympic games. It's Norway's oldest winter-sports resort where you'll will find plenty to do. There are Olympic venues, museums, boutiques, and restaurants.

To reach it from Oslo, trains leave Central Station every hour. The trip takes nearly two-and-a-half hours. The cost is approximately NOK440, but cheaper if purchased in advance. For tickets, check out the NSB train website at www.nsb.no. Trains also leave Oslo's Gardermoen airport hourly. If you're driving, the main route is on highway E6. It's 115 miles (185 km) from Oslo to Lillehammer. Bus operators Bussekspress (www.nor-way.no. From NOK500)and Nettbus (www.nettbus.no. From NOK280) depart from Oslo's main bus station and from Gardermoen airport.

If you arrive by train or bus at Lillehammer Station, the main shopping street **Storgata** ("Big Street") is only a few blocks away and is lined with shops and restaurants in attractive wooden houses.

If you're coming here to ski, you'll find 217 miles (350 km) of cross-country ski trails at Sjusjøen and Nordseter. The excellent ski center at Hafjell is only 15 minutes away by bus.

Check out the destination's informative website at en.lillehammer.com.

Top sights include:

Maihaugen: Northern Europe's largest open-air museum has 200 traditional Norwegian buildings, everything from a stave church from the 1200s to a 1980s typical Norwegian home.

Norwegian Olympic Museum: An interactive museum with a heavy emphasis on both the 1994 Lillehammer games and the 1952 Winter Olympics in Oslo.

Lillehammer Art Museum: Housed in a striking modern building, the museum features over 1500 works dating from the 19th century, focusing on Norwegian contemporary art.

Lysgårdsbakkene Ski Jumping Arena: This was the ski-jumping venue for the 1994 Olympics. Today, it's a year-round attraction with a chairlift to the top. You can also hike the 954 steps to the top.

Lillehammer Olympic Bob and Luge Track: The Bob and Luge Track was one of the venues for the 1994 Olympics. During summer and winter, you can experience what it's like to speed down the track.

Winter Olympic Powerhouse

Norway has won more medals in the Winter Olympic Games than any other nation. More than half of these medals have come from cross-country skiing and speed skating.

Norway is one of only three nations (along with Austria and Liechtenstein) to have won more medals at the Winter Games than at the Summer Games.

Excursion to Oslofjord

The narrow straits of the **Oslofjord** link the city with the sea. This waterway is about 60 miles long and is the country's busiest. This fjord is nothing like the dramatic fjords found in other parts of the country. If your time is limited (and you're not going to head out to areas like Bergen), you may want to take a ferry ride to check out the Oslofjord. While fjords in other parts of the country are pristine, this fjord is a center of commerce and there are many industrial complexes.

On the western side of the fjord, you can visit **Tønsberg**, Norway's oldest city. To reach the area by car, it's a 65-mile trip on route E18. The train ride from Oslo's Central Station on NSB (www.nsb.no) takes about 90 minutes (the train departs in the direction of Larvik). You can also reach the city by bus from the Oslo Bus Terminal. Tønsberg was founded by the Vikings, and is home to the Viking burial mounds. Stroll along the main harbor, visit the wharf, view a Viking ship at the Slottsfjell Museum, or check out a surprising collection of modern art (including Andy Warhol paintings) at the Haugar Vestfold Art Museum.

Drøbak is an attractive village on the fjord's east shore located at its narrowest point. It's popular with day-trippers, as it's just a 40-minute drive (along route E6) from Oslo. There are plenty of sightseeing boats that depart from the waterfront in Oslo. For budget travelers, there are frequent departures by bus at the Oslo Bus Terminal, and the trip will take about an hour.

Past Drøbak along the eastern shore of the fjord is **Fredrikstad**. The 60-mile drive here along route E6 takes about an hour. You can also take an NSB train (www.nsb.no) from Central Station in Oslo. Trains leave hourly (in the direction of Göteborg or Halden), and the trip takes about an hour. The town is located near the border with Sweden. You can also take a bus from the Oslo Bus Terminal and the ride takes about 90 minutes.

The old town of Fredrikstad has an incredibly preserved fortress which was built to defend the country from the Swedes. Old Town, with its cobblestone streets, is accessible by taking a short ferry across the river from the train station.

BERGEN RAILWAY

The Bergen Railway is Northern Europe's highest stretch of railway.

The 310-mile route connects Oslo and Bergen, and takes about seven hours. Construction of the railway was an incredible engineering project. Begun in 1893 and completed 16 years later, the trip is considered to be one of the world's most scenic train rides. There are four daily departures from Oslo and Bergen. The trip takes you across one of Europe's highest mountain plateaus, and to some of Norway's best natural attractions.

The train is comfortable, timely, and clean (as are all trains in Norway). There's a bar and cafe on board. If you prefer to travel in the evening, the Bergen Railway operates a night train with sleeping compartments, but you'll miss the breathtaking scenery.

At the Myrdal stop, you can take a detour to the **Flåm Railway**. The Flåm Railway is one of the world's steepest railway journeys, and takes you through spectacular scenery down steep mountain trails.

Reservations can be made at www.nsb.no. The one-way cost of the trip is from NOK500. Off season is significantly less. You can only purchase tickets online three months ahead of time.

Norway's most popular tour is "Norway in a Nutshell." The tour includes the scenic Bergen Railway, the Flåm Railway, fjord cruise, and a bus tour. For more information on this and other fjord tours see www.fjordtours.com. From NOK1600.

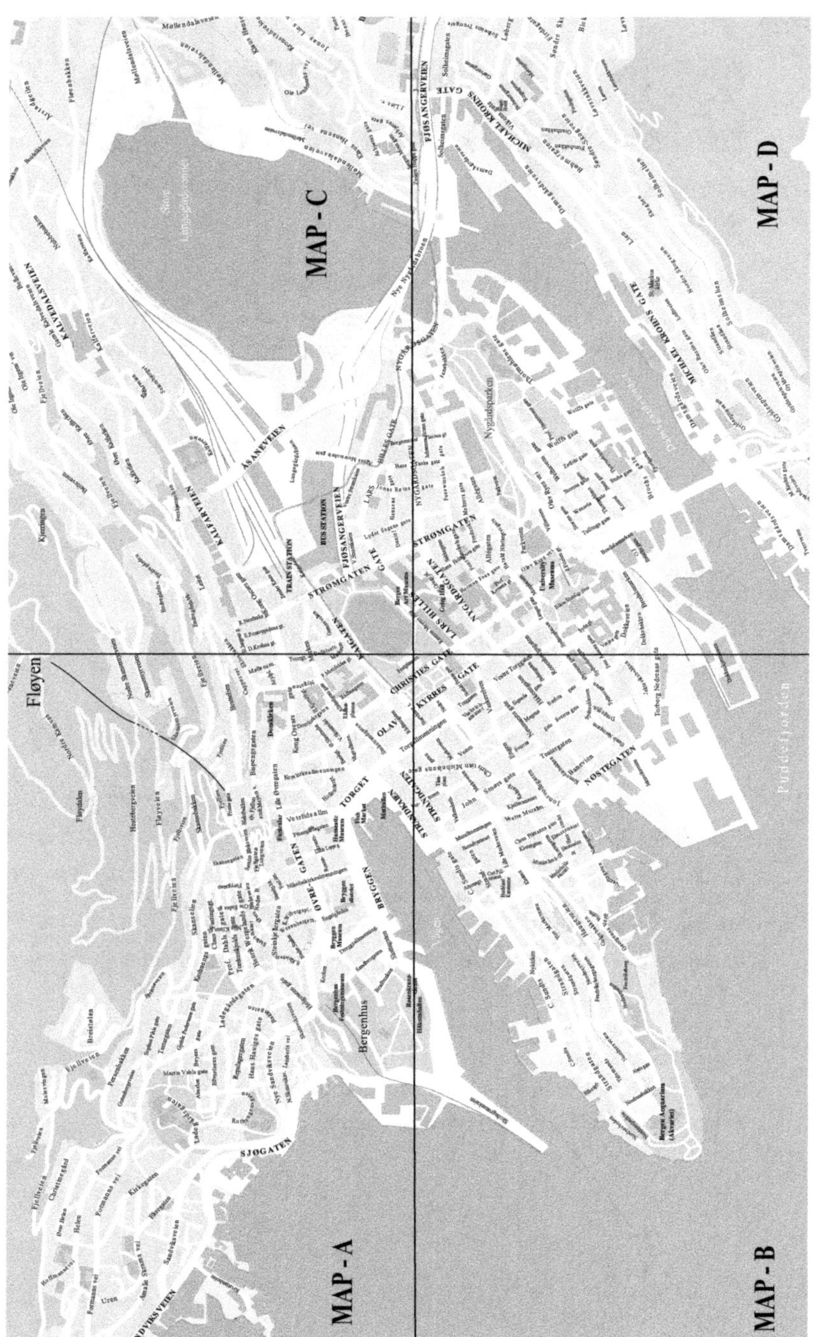

MAP - A
MAP - B
MAP - C
MAP - D
Fløyen
Bergenhus
SJØGATEN
SANDVIKSVEIEN
KALVEDALSVEIEN
NYHAVNSVEIEN
ÅSANEVEIEN
FJØSANGERVEIEN
STRØMGATEN
STRØMGATEN GATE
LARS HILLES GATE
NYGÅRDSGATEN
MICHAEL KROHNS GATE
FJØSANGERVEIEN GATE
CHRISTIES GATE
KONG OSCARS GATE
OLAV KYRRES GATE
TORGET
ØVREGATEN
BRYGGEN
STRANDGATEN
NØSTEGATEN
BUS STATION
TRAIN STATION
Puddefjorden

BERGEN: TOP SIGHTS

- **Market Square**
The picturesque fish market has been here since
the 1200s.

- **Hanseatic Wharf**
Colorful wooden warehouses line the harbor.

- **Bryggen district**
Stroll through the old quarter, with narrow alleyways filled
with souvenir stores, workshops, restaurants, and boutiques.

- **Bryggen Museum**
Bergen's oldest building, dating back to the 1100s, houses this
archeological museum.

- **Bergenhus Fortress**
This imposing fortress has stood at the entrance to the harbor
since the late 16th century.

- **Cathedral (Domkirken)**
Bergen's main church features a Rococo interior and magnificent stained-glass windows.

- **Mount Floyen and the Funicular**
Fantastic panoramic views of Bergen and the surrounding area.

- **Grieg Hall (Grieghallen)**
This modern concert hall is named in honor of Bergen-born
composer Edvard Grieg

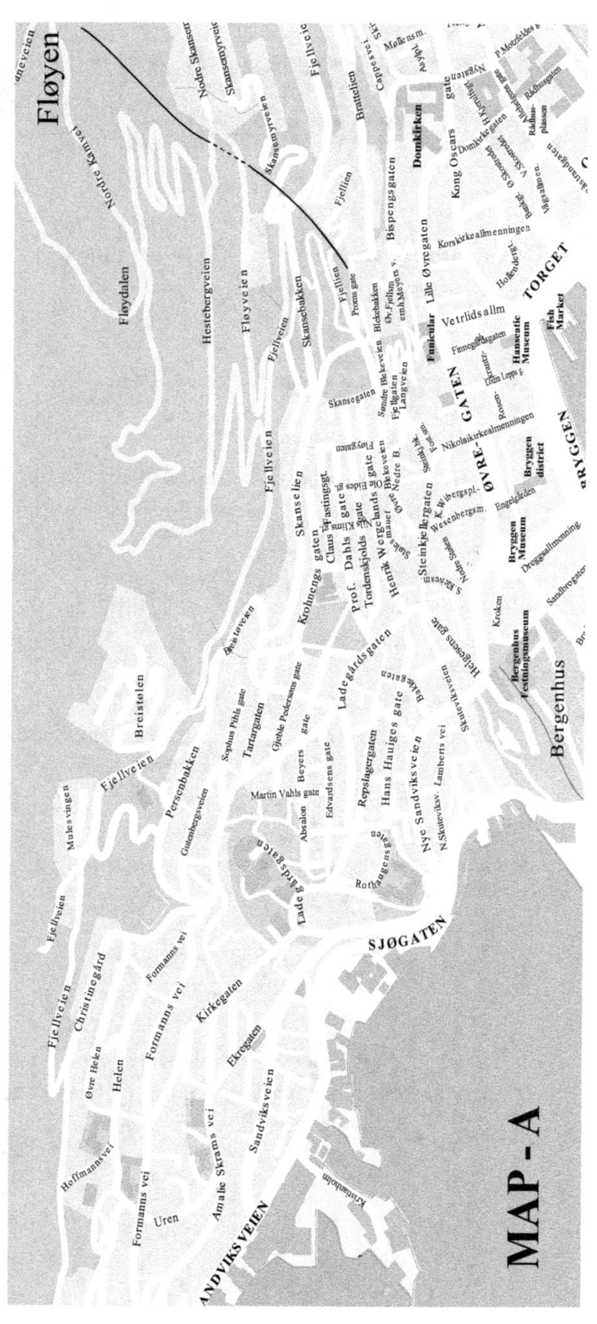

Fløyen
Fjellveien
Nødre Skanser
Skansemyrveien
Skansemyrveien
Brattelien
Cappesvei
Møllen sm.
Asylpl.
Nygaten
P. Motzfeldts
Domkirken
Bispengsgaten
Kong Oscars gate
Domkirkegaten
Radhus-
plassen
Nødre Kanvei
Fjellien
Øv.Fjellsm. v.
enh.Meyers v.
Korskirkeallmenningen
Hollender v.
TORGET
Fløydalen
Hestebergveien
Fløyveien
Fjellveien
Skansebakken
Fjellien
Prøms gate
Bleiebakken
Søndre Bekkeven
Langveien
Lille Øvregaten
Funicular
Vetrlidsallm
Finnegårdsgaten
Hanseatic
Museum
Fish
Market
Skansegaten
Fjellgaten
Skanselien
Fjellveien
Fløygaten
Ole Eides gate
Øvre Bekkeven
Øvre Nedre B.
Nikolaikirkeallmenningen
ØVRE-GATEN
Bryggen
district
Skanselien
Claus Fastingsgt.
Kohnengs gaten
Prof. Dahls gate
Tordenskjolds gate
Henrik Wergelands gate
Klims gate
Steinkjellergaten
K.Wibergspl.
Wesenbergsm.
Engelgården
Bryggen
Museum
Dreggsallmenning
Sandbrogaten
Øgstuveien
Ladegårdsgaten
s.Ravesm.
Nødre Sogen
Kroken
Bergenhus
Festningsmuseum
Breistølen
Sophus Pihls gate
Tartargaten
Gjeble Pedersans gate
gate
Bakkegaten
Helgesens gate
Skuteviksveien
Bergenhus
Fjellveien
Mulesvingen
Persenbakken
Gutenbergsveien
Martin Vahls gate
Absalon
Edvardsens gate
Repslagergaten
Hans Hauges gate
Nye Sandviksveien
N.Skuteviksv. Lamberts vei
Rothaugens gaten
Rothe
Fjellveien
Christinegård
Formanns vei
Kirkegaten
Ladegårdsgaten
SJØGATEN
Øvr. Helen
Helen
Formanns vei
Ekregaten
Sandviksveien
Fjellveien
Hoffmannsvei
Formanns vei
Uren
Amalie Skrams vei
Kristinholm
SANDVIKSVEIEN
MAP - A
BRYGGEN

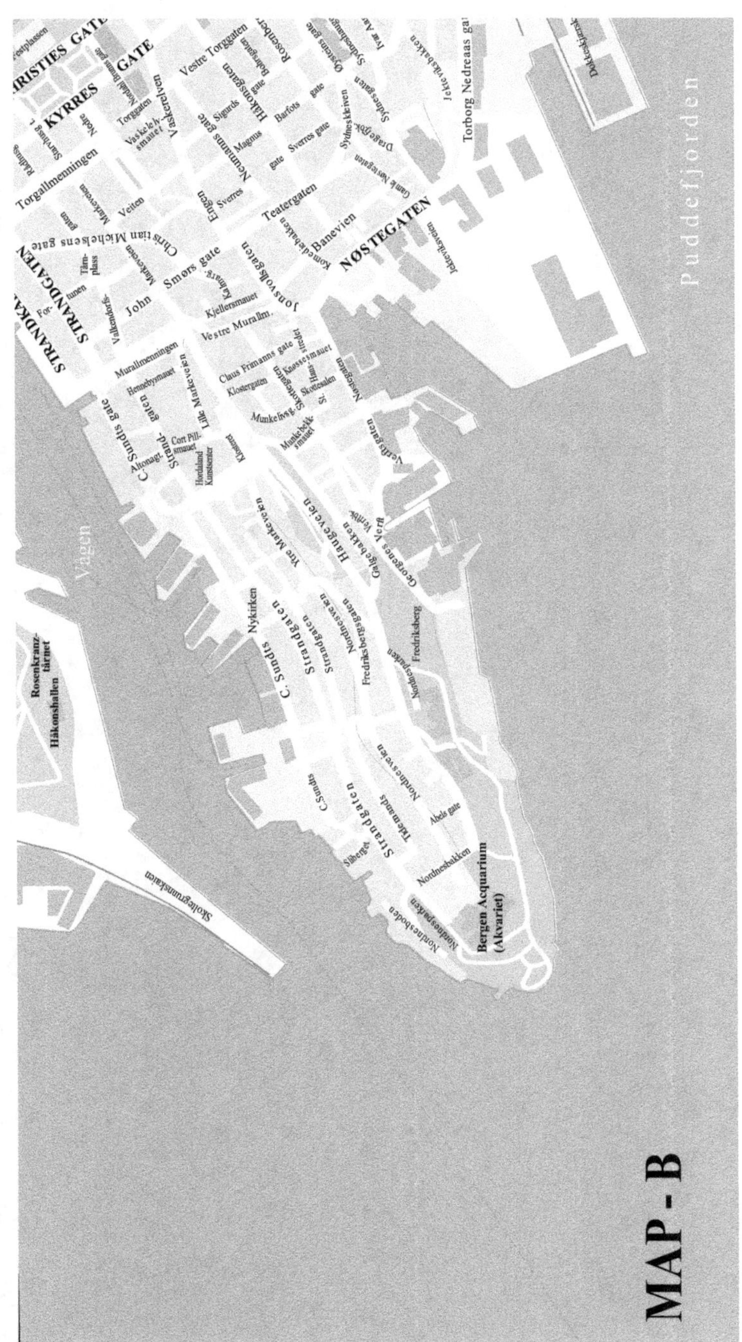
KRISTIES GATE
KYRRES GATE
Torgallmenningen
STRANDGATEN
Christian Michelsens gate
Smørs gate
Vestre Torggaten
Håkonsgaten
Sigurds gate
Magnus gate
Sverres gate
Barfots gate
Teatergaten
Banevien
NØSTEGATEN
Kjellersmauet
Vestre Murallm.
Claus Frimanns gate
Klostergaten
Murallmenningen
Hennebysmauet
Lille Markevien
C. Sundts gate
Strand-gaten
Altonagt.
Cort Piil-smauet
Hordaland Kunstsenter
Kjøpet
Ytre Markevien
Haugeveien
Georgenes Verft
Nykirken
C. Sundts
Strandgaten
Strandgaten
Fredriksberggaten
Fredriksberg
Nordnespaken
Vågen
Rosenkranz-tårnet
Håkonshallen
Skolegrunnskaien
C. Sundts
Strandgaten
Tikemands
Sibenget
Nordnesbakken
Nordnesparken
Nordnesboden
Bergen Acquarium
(Akvariet)
Abels gate
Nordnesveien
Puddefjorden
Torborg Nedreaas gate
MAP - B

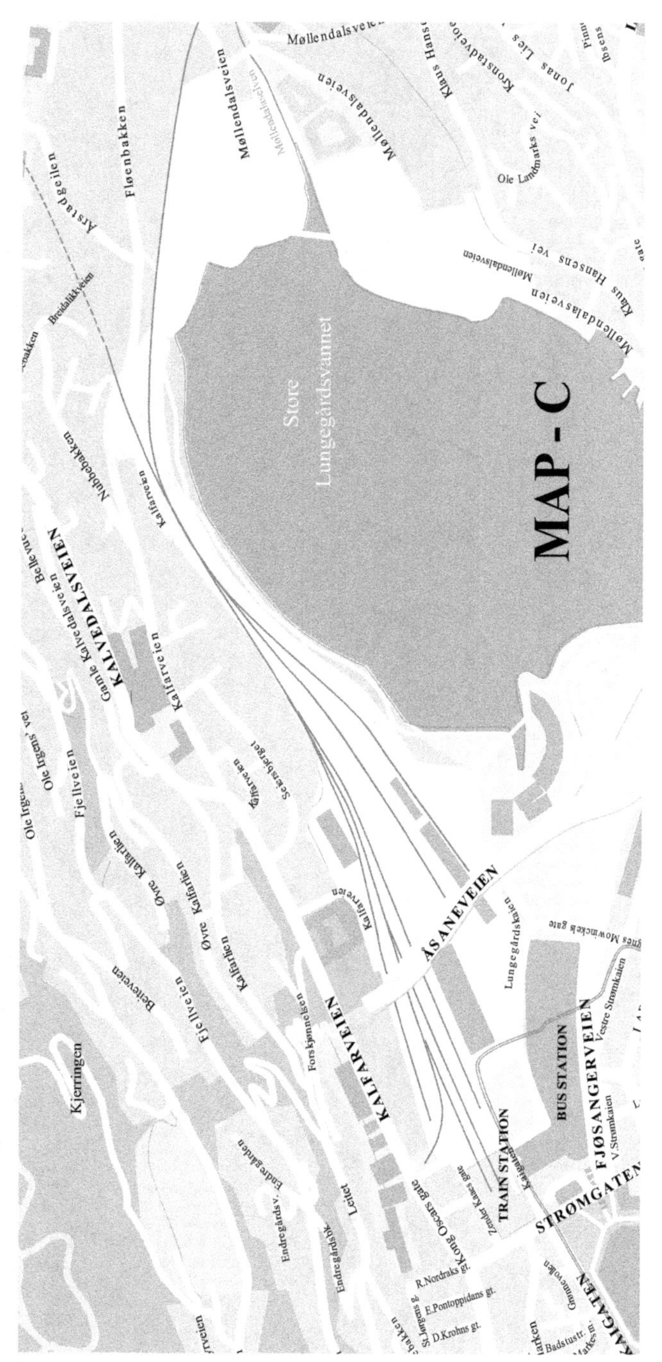
Møllendalsveien
Klaus Hansens
Kronstadveien
Jonas Lies
fbsens
Fløenbakken
Møllendalsveien
Møllendalsveien
Møllendalsveien
Ole Landmarks vei
Arstadgeilen
Breidalikkveien
Klaus Hansens vei
Møllendalsveien
Møllendalsveien
Store
Lungegårdsvannet
MAP - C
Nubbebakken
Kalfarveien
Belleveien
Gamle Kalvedalsveien
KALVEDALSVEIEN
Kalfarveien
Kalfarveien
Ole Ingens' vei
Ole Ingens
Fjellveien
Sverresbjerget
Kjøttveien
Øvre Kalfarlien
Kalfarlien
Kalfarveien
Fjellveien
Beltveien
ÅSANEVEIEN
Lungegårdskaien
Mowinckels gate
Kjerringen
Fjellveien
Forskjønnelsen
KALFARVEIEN
Vestre Strømkaien
BUS STATION
FJØSANGERVEIEN
V.Strømkaien
Endregårdsveien
Endregårdsbk
Leitet
TRAIN STATION
STRØMGATEN
Kong Oscars gate
Fridtof Nans gate
R.Nordraks gt.
St.Jørgens g.
E.Pontoppidans gt.
D.Krohns gt.
Badstustr.
KAIGATEN

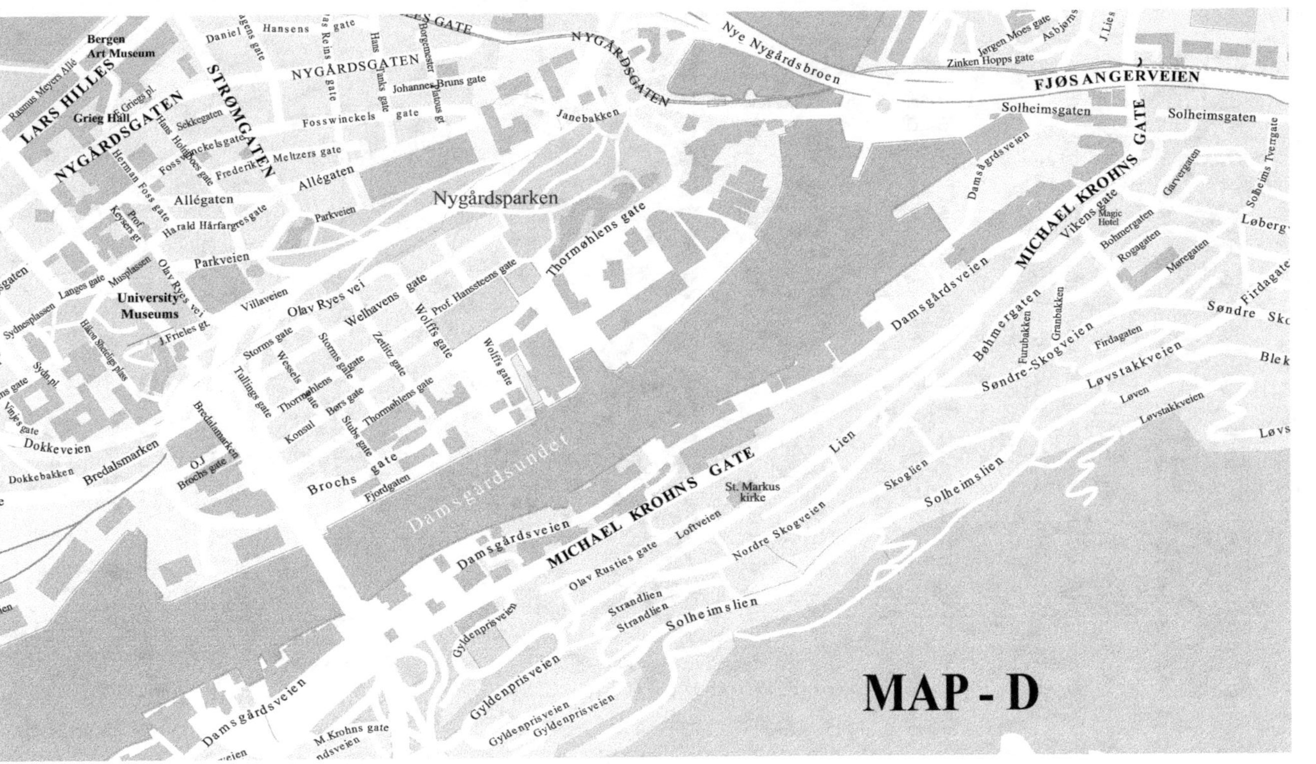
MAP - D
Bergen Art Museum
LARS HILLES
Grieg Hall
NYGÅRDSGATEN
STRØMGATEN
NYGÅRDSGATEN
Rasmus Meyers Allé
Griegs pl.
Daniel Hansens gate
as Reins gate
Hans Tanks gate
Borgemester
Johannes Bruns gate
Blatous gt
GATE
Nye Nygårdsbroen
Jørgen Moes gate
Asbjørns
J. Lies
Zinken Hopps gate
FJØSANGERVEIEN
Solheimsgaten
Solheimsgaten
Damsgårdsveien
MICHAEL KROHNS GATE
Vikens gate
Magic Hotel
Bohmergaten
Rogngaten
Garverigaten
Solheims Tverrgate
Løberg
Møregaten
Firdagate
Sekkegaten
Fosswinckels gate
Janebakken
Hans Holmboes gate
Meltzers gate
Herman Foss gate
Fosswinckelsgate
Frederikke
Allégaten
Allégaten
Parkveien
Nygårdsparken
Thormøhlens gate
Damsgårdsveien
Bøhmergaten
Furubakken
Grønbakken
Søndre-Skogveien
Firdagaten
Søndre Sko
Løvstakkveien
Blek
Prof. Keysers gt
Harald Hårfargesgate
Parkveien
Villaveien
Olav Ryes vei
Welhavens gate
Wolffs gate
Prof. Hansteens gate
Damsgårdsveien
Løven
Løvstakkveien
Løvs
University Museums
sgaten
Langes gate
Muséplassen
Olav Ryes vei
Storms gate
Storms gate
Wellhavens
Zetlitz gate
Wolffs gate
Wolffs gate
Lien
Skoglien
Solheimslien
Sydnesplassen
Håkon Sheteligs plass
J. Frieles gt.
Wessels gate
Thormøhlens gate
Børs gate
Thormøhlens gate
St. Markus kirke
Syd n pl.
Vinjes gate
Tullings gate
Konsul
Stubs gate
Brochs gate
Fjordgaten
Damsgårdsundet
MICHAEL KROHNS GATE
Nordre Skogveien
Solheimslien
Dokkeveien
Dokkebakken
Bredalsmarken
O.J Brochs gate
Bredalsmarken
Damsgårdsveien
Olav Rusties gate
Loftveien
Strandlien
Strandlien
Solheimslien
Damsgårdsveien
M.Krohns gate
ndsveien
Gyldenprisveien
Gyldenprisveien
Gyldenprisveien
Gyldenprisveien

BERGEN

Scenic Bergen is the country's second largest city and Norway's busiest port for cruise ships. The city's stunning setting and picturesque natural harbor make this destination one of Norway's most popular tourist attractions.

Situated on the west coast of the country, Bergen is home to 300,000 residents. It's located on the Bergenshalvøyen peninsula, and is surrounded by seven mountains.

Bergen is the most popular gateway to the fjords of West Norway. It's also one of Europe's most popular destinations for hiking. Most of Bergen's top sights are located within easy walking distance of each other.

City of Festivals

Bergen is known for its festivals and is also home to one of Europe's oldest orchestras, the **Bergen Philharmonic Orchestra**, founded in 1765.
www.harmonien.no.

The most popular festivals are:

- **Nattjazz Festival** (late May/early June) One of Europe's largest jazz festivals.
www.nattjazz.no.
- **Bergenfest** (mid-June) Music festival with an eclectic lineup featuring international artists.
www.bergenfest.no.
- **Bergen International Festival** (May-June) 300 events over two weeks, with music, theater, dance, opera, and performing arts.
www.fib.no.

Market Square/Bryggen District/ Hanseatic Wharf

The fish market (**Torget**) has been here since the 1200s. It's a perfect place to sample fresh seafood. Get your camera out, as the picturesque market offers plenty of opportunities to photograph the colorful food and flowers. In 2012 the indoor Fish Market (Mathallen) opened, where shops and restaurants are open all year.

The market area is surrounded by buildings dating back to the 1700s and 1800s. These colorful wooden warehouses of the **Bryggen district** and **Hanseatic Wharf** line the harbor. Nearby you can stroll through the old quarter, with narrow alleyways filled with souvenir stores, workshops, restaurants, and boutiques.

Info: 1 Grensegrenden. Open daily. Admission: Free.

Hanseatic Museum

Finnegård is one of the 18th-century merchant homes in the Bryggen district. It has housed the Hanseatic Museum since 1872. You'll experience what life in the harbor area was like for German merchants (the Hanseatics) who lived here. On display are weapons, equipment, and furnishings (including the tiny beds of the migrant workers who lived here).

Info: 1a Finnegården. Tel. 53 00 61 10. Open daily Jan-Apr and Oct-Dec 11am-3pm, May and Sep 9am-5pm, Jun-Aug 9am-6pm. Admission: NOK120. www.museumvest.no.

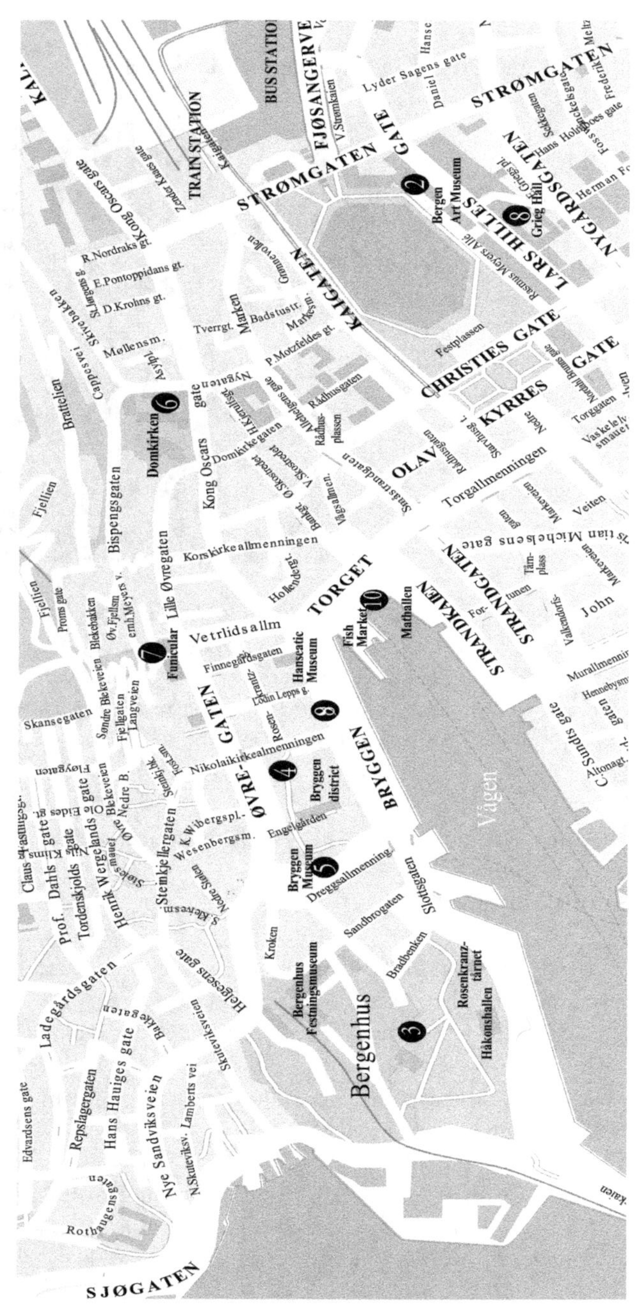
KALV
KONG OSCARS gate
Zander Kaaes gate
R.Nordraks gt.
E.Pontoppidans gt.
D.Krohns gt.
Sl.Langens g.
Cappes vei
Skytterbakken
Møllensm.
Brattelien
Fjellien
Asylpl.
Bispengsgaten
Domkirken
Kong Oscars gate
Domkirke gaten
Nygaten
H.K.Krohns gt.
Allehelgens gate
P.Motzfeldes gt.
Rådhus-
gaten
V.Skostredet
Ø.Skostredet
Bendix
Vågsallmen.
Vågsbunn.
Rådhus-
plassen
Småstrandgaten
Fjellien
Proms gate
Øv.Fjellsm.
e.m.Meyers v.
Blekebakken
Funicular
Lille Øvregaten
Vetrlidsallm
Finnegårdsgaten
Hanseatic
Museum
TORGET
Fish
Market
Mathallen
STRANDKAIEN
STRANDGATEN
For-
tunen
Tårn-
plass
John
Valkendorfs
Murallmenn
Hennebysm
TRAIN STATION
Kreuergaten
Grønnevollen
STRØMGATEN
V.Strømkaien
FJØSANGERVE
BUS STATION
KAIGATEN
GATE
Bergen
Art Museum
Lyder Sagens gate
Daniel gate
STRØMGATEN
Grieg Hall
Grieg pl.
LARS HILLES
Rasmus Meyers Allé
NYGÅRDS
GATE
Hans Holmboes gate
Sakkegaten
Fosswinckelsgate
Frederiksgt.
Herman F
Festplassen
CHRISTIES GATE
KYRRES
GATE
OLAV
Nedre
Strandsg.
Torgallmenningen
Veiten
Markeveien
stian Michelsens gate
Torggaten
Vaskelv
smauet
Nedre Korskirke allmenning
Hollendergt.
Mathveien
Markeveien
TORGET
BRYGGEN
Vågen
C.Sundts gate
Altonagt.
Sondre Blekeveien
Fjellgaten
Langveien
Skansegaten
Fløygaten
Ole Eides gt.
Nils Klims gate
Øvre Blekeveien
Nedre B.
Festsm.
Stølesm.
Steinkjk.
ÅVRE-
GATEN
GATEN
Rosen-
Lodin Lepps g.
L.Frantz
Nikolaikirkealmenningen
Engelgården
Bryggen
district
Bryggen
Museum
Dreggsallmenning
BRYGGEN
Slottsgaten
Sandbrogaten
Bradbenken
Rosenkranz-
tårnet
Håkonshallen
Bergenhus
Festningsmuseum
Bergenhus
Kroken
Claus Fastings gate
Prof. Dahls gate
Tordenskjolds gate
Henrik Werglands gate
K.Wibergspl.
Wesenbergsm.
Stemkjellergaten
Nedre Stølen
S.Klæbersm.
Ladegårdsgaten
Bakkegaten
Heljesens gate
Edvardsens gate
Repslagergaten
Hans Hauiges gate
Nye Sandviksveien
Skutevikksveien
N.Skuteviksv. Lamberts vei
N.Sugrugensgaten
Roth
SJØGATEN
katen

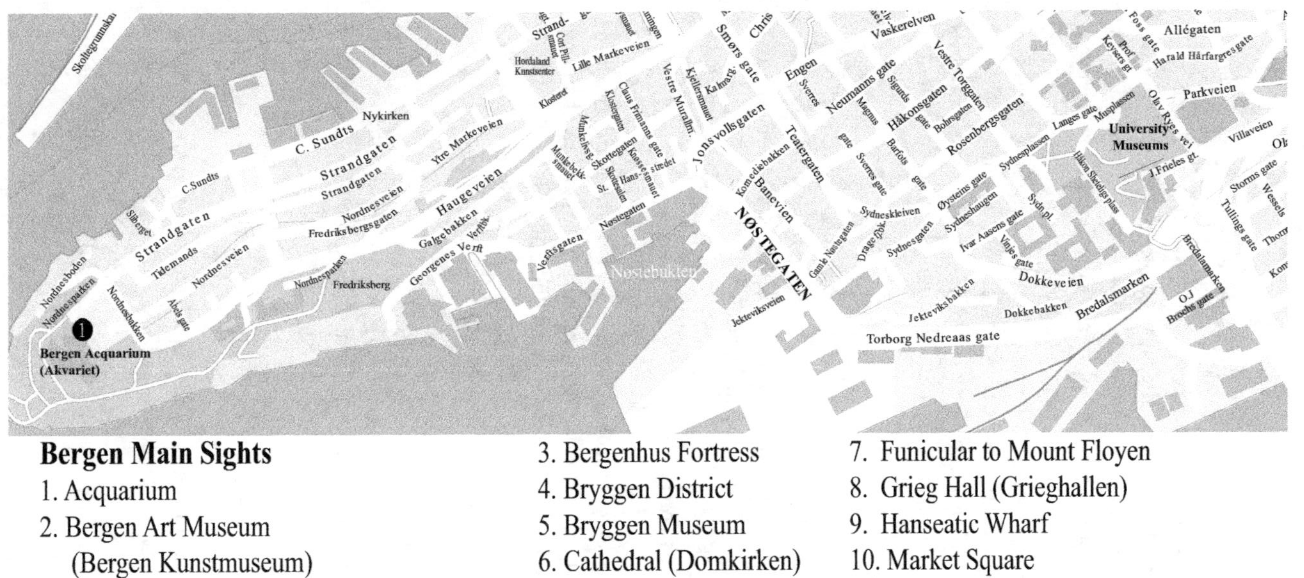

Bergen Main Sights

1. Acquarium
2. Bergen Art Museum
   (Bergen Kunstmuseum)

3. Bergenhus Fortress
4. Bryggen District
5. Bryggen Museum
6. Cathedral (Domkirken)

7. Funicular to Mount Floyen
8. Grieg Hall (Grieghallen)
9. Hanseatic Wharf
10. Market Square

Bryggen Museum

The Bryggen district has been an important part of Bergen since the Middle Ages. The area is on the UNESCO World Heritage List. In 1955 parts of Bryggen were destroyed in a fire. The excavation that took place after the destruction uncovered thousands of objects which give an insight into life in the city in the Middle Ages. The museum opened in 1976, houses these archaeological materials, and is built on the remains of Bergen's oldest building dating back to the 1100s. Temporary exhibits feature Norwegian paintings, photographs, and household goods.

Info: Bryggen. Tel. 55 30 80 30. Open mid-Sep to mid-May daily 11am-3pm, mid-May to mid-Sep daily 9am-4pm. Admission: NOK100. Free entrance to the Museum Shop and the Museum Cafè. www.bymuseet.no.

Bergenhus Fortress

The imposing Bergenhus Fortress has stood at the entrance to the harbor since the late 16th century. Also here are the remains of Sverresborg, a fortress built around 1660 on the remains of a 12th-century castle. The Bergenhus Fortress Museum tells the story of the resistance movement during the 1940-45 Nazi occupation.

Info: Bergenhus. Open Jan-Apr Tue-Sun 11am-5pm, closed Mon. Apr-Oct daily 11am-5pm. Closed Nov-Dec. Admission: Free.

Håkon's Hall and the Rosenkrantz Tower

Bergenhus fortress is located at the end of Bryggen wharf. Here you'll find both **Håkon's Hall** and the **Rosenkrantz Tower**.

Norwegian King Håkon Håkonsson built this royal residence

and banquet hall in 1261. For years, the hall (with its thick stone walls) was used as a warehouse. It's been restored and is used once again for ceremonial events; it's also a popular venue for concerts.

Next to the hall is Rosenkrantz Tower, and is the most important Renaissance monument in Norway. Parts of the structure date back to 1270. You can climb its narrow stairs to the roof where you'll find panoramic views of the harbor and surrounding mountains. The basement houses a former dungeon which remained in use until the early 19th century.

Info: Bergenhus Festning. Tel. 55 30 80 30. Open mid-Sep to mid-May daily noon-3pm. Open mid-May to mid-Sep daily 10am-4pm. When either Håkon's Hall or Rosenkrantz Tower is closed, the other is open. Admission: NOK100. www. bymuseet.no.

Cathedral (Domkirken)

It's amazing that Bergen's cathedral is still here: It has burned down five times over the years. The first church was built in the mid-12th century. It was then, and continues to be today, dedicated to Olav the Holy, the patron saint of Norway.

The building you see today dates from the 1880s, when a Rococo interior and magnificent stained-glass windows with biblical motifs were added, including the birth of Jesus, crucifixion, resurrection, and baptism by John. All that remains from the 13th century are the Gothic choir stalls, and a cannonball has been embedded in the west wall since the Battle of Bergen in 1665.

Info: Kong Oscargate and Domkirkegate. Tel. 55 59 71 75. Open daily. Admission: Free. *Currently closed for renovations.*

Mount Floyen and the Funicular

If you want to experience panoramic views of Bergen and the surrounding islands, you can take the funicular from the city center to the top of Mount Floyen. You'll be over 1000 feet (320 meters) above sea level. Trails offer easy hiking through beautiful woodlands, including the stunning, peaceful, and secluded lake here. Not to be missed!

There's a souvenir shop, cafe, and gourmet restaurant **Ulriken 643** (Restaurant: Tel. 45 90 89 62. www.ulriken643.no).

Info: Departure point is near the Fish Market in the center of Bergen. Tel. 55 33 68 00. The funicular runs every day, all year round. Mon-Fri 7:30am-11pm, Sat and Sun 8am-11pm. Admission: Round-trip NOK100. www.floyen.no.

Grieg Hall
(Grieghallen)

Norway is known for its modern architecture. This 1,500-seat concert hall is named in honor of Bergen-born composer Edvard Grieg, who once served as music director of the Bergen Philharmonic Orchestra. It's now the orchestra's home. The structure was designed by the Danish architect Knud Munk in 1967, and was completed in 1978. The hall is famous for its acoustics, and hosts concerts, operas, and ballets.

Info: Edvard Griegs Plass. Tel. 55 21 61 00 (ticket office). www.grieghallen.no.

Bergen Art Museum (KODE)
(Bergen Kunstmuseum)

The KODE Museums include the Stenersens Collection, Rasmus Meyers Collection, and Lysverket Collection. The museums are all located next to each other in four buildings.

• Stenersens Collection is a contemporary-art collection. You'll find modern art from such notables as Diego Rivera, Joan Miró, and Pablo Picasso. The history of the Bergen Avant Garde scene from 1966 to 1985 is also explored.

• Rasmus Meyers Collection contains Norwegian art from the 18th century to 1915, including works by Edvard Munch, J.C. Dahl, and Nikolai Astrup.

• Lysverket Art Collection features Norwegian and foreign art from the 1400s until the 20th century.

• The Museum of Decorative Art has a collection of rare porcelain, pottery, goldsmith work, and decorative art.

All told, the KODE collection includes 50,000 works of art. In addition to the works in the city center, the museum also displays its collection in the homes of the composers Ole Bull, Harald Sæverud, and Edvard Grieg.

Info: 3/7 Rasmus Meyers Alle 3/7. Tel. 55 56 80 00. Open mid-Sep to mid- May Tue–Fri 11am–4pm, Sat and Sun 11am-5pm. Closed Mon. Mid-May to mid-Sep Tue-Sun 10am-5pm. Closed Mon. Admission: NOK130 in the winter and NOK 160 in the summer (access to all museums in the complex). www.kodebergen.no.

Old Bergen
(Gamle Bergen)

Norway is famous for its open-air museums. This one features 55 wooden buildings dating back to the 18th and 19th centuries. These structures originally were located in the center of the city. In the 1800s, Bergen had the largest collection of wooden structures in Europe. You can take a guided tour or walk around on your own, and experience what life was like in Bergen. The museum features special events, especially in summer.

Info: 4 Nyhavnsveien (in the Sandviken district). Tel. 55 30 80 30. Open daily mid-May to mid-Sep 10am-4pm. Admission: NOK120. Under 16 free. www.bymuseet.no.

Bergen Aquarium
(Akvariet)

There are 50 aquariums here (nine large aquariums, 42 smaller tanks, and three outdoor pools). Especially popular are the exhibits with seals and penguins.

The museum features a large-format film about the world below sea level. The film stresses the importance of oceans to society, and the dangers of water pollution (especially plastic waste). Note that this sight is quite expensive (even for Norway!). The aquarium is reached on foot in about 20 minutes from Bergen's main square to the end of the Nordnes peninsula. You can also take Skyss bus number 11 from the central city.

Info: Tel. 55 55 71 71. Open Sep-Apr 10am-6pm, May-Aug 9am-6pm. Admission: NOK295, children 3-15 NOK180. Family (2 adults and 2 children NOK810). www.akvariet.no.

**University Museums
(Universitetsmuseet i Bergen)**

The university museums include the **Natural History Collection**, the **Cultural History Collection**, and the **Seafaring Museum**. Also here is the **Botanic Garden**. The Norwegian Arboretum has a first-rate collection of over 5,000 plants from around the world.

Info: 3 Museplass. Tel. 55 58 29 20. Museums: Tue-Sat 10am-4pm, Sun 11am-5pm. Closed Mon. Museum garden: Sep-May daily 6:30am-6pm, Jun-Aug 6:30am-8pm. Admission: NOK120. www.uib.no/en/universitymuseum. *The Greenhouse is currently closed for renovations.*

Troldhaugen/Grieg Museum

The former villa of Norwegian composer Edvard Grieg and his wife Nina is located in Troldhaugen (south of Bergen). Built in 1885, his home is now the site of the Grieg Museum, dedicated to the composer's life and work.

Bergen Area

Bergen Central City
Troldhaugen
Airport
Light Rail (Skyss)
Fana
Lysøen
E39
580
553
555
555
558
557
540
556
582
582
585
553
546
556
Grimstadfjorden
Puddefjorden
Fanafjorden

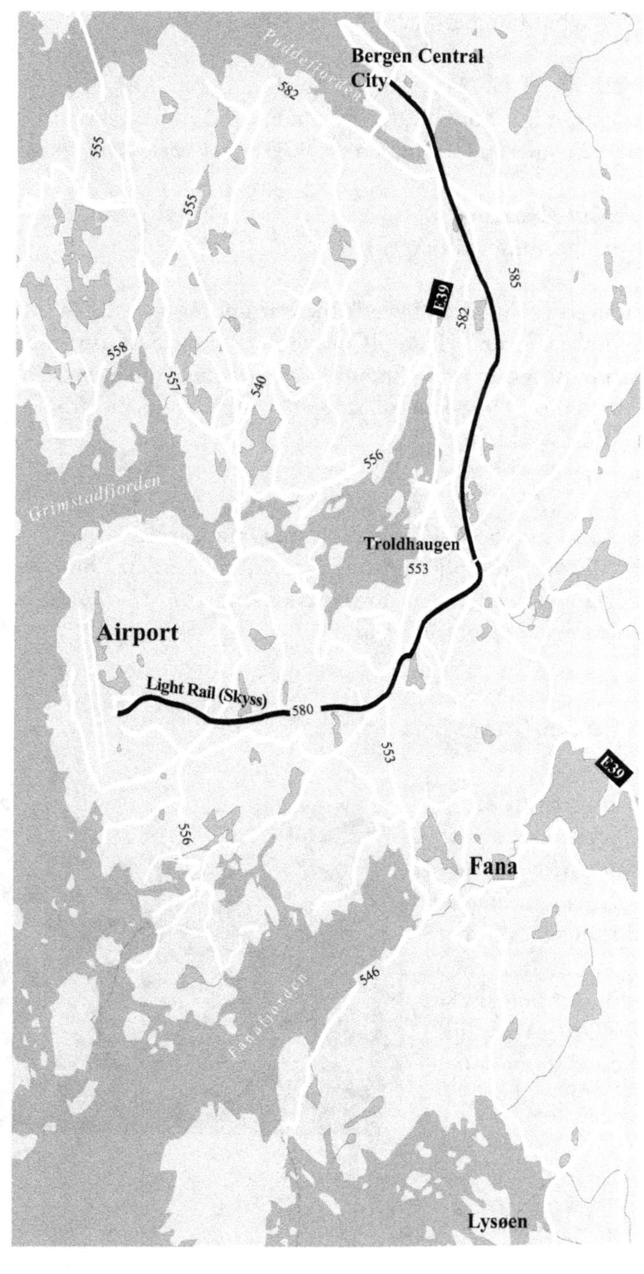

Among his possessions on display are Grieg's Steinway piano from 1892. Also here is Troldsalen, a chamber-music hall that seats 200 people, where frequent concerts are held (concert schedule at the museum website).

Info: 65 Troldhaugvegen. Tel. 55 92 29 92. Open Oct-Apr 10am-4pm, May-Sep 9am-6pm. Admission: NOK130, under 16 free. www.griegmuseum.no.

Arrival in Bergen

The modern, efficient, and clean Bergen Airport (BGO) is located 10 miles (16 kilometers) from the central city.

A **taxi** costs about NOK400-500 to the city center (up to double if you are traveling in the early morning or late evening).

The **light rail** (Skyss) stop is right outside the terminal. Tickets for the Light Rail can be bought at the stop or at the ticket machine at the baggage claim area (credit cards accepted). Cost: NOK38 (NOK60 if purchased on board).

The **Airport Express bus** stops outside the main terminal. The bus drives an express route that takes 30 minutes to the Bergen Bus Station. In the city center the bus also stops at Festplassen and Bryggen, with departures every 10 minutes during the day. Extremely convenient!

The bus operates Monday to Friday 6:50am to 8:00pm (every 10 minutes), 8:10pm to 10:30pm (every 20 minutes), and 11:10pm to 4:00am (every hour).

Saturday 7:00am to 7:30pm (every 30 minutes), 8:00am to 7:45pm (every 15 minutes), and 8:00pm to 2:05am (every 30 minutes).

Sunday 4:50 am to 11:30am (approximately every 30 minutes, midday to midnight (every 10 minutes), after midnight (approximately every hour and a half).

One-way ticket fare: NOK119.

You can purchase your ticket at the Bergen Airport bus booths in the Arrivals Hall or on board from the driver (for an extra fee of NOK30).

The **local bus** stop is also outside the terminal building. Bus number 23 to Straume (Sotra) stops in the city center. Operates from 7:06 am to 4:55pm (every 30 minutes). Ticket is purchased on the bus and is slightly less than the Airport Express bus.

ICE BAR

Magic Ice

You'll be given a warm poncho and gloves when you visit this bar, gallery, and souvenir shop. You'll need them, as you'll be surrounded by ice sculptures at this indoor winter wonderland.

Info: 50 C. Sundts gate. Tel. 93.00.80.23. Open daily at 4pm in winter, 11am in summer. Admission: NOK225 (includes one drink). www.magicice.no.

DINING IN BERGEN

Get ready to eat a lot of seafood in Bergen. You'll find dishes such as *fiskesuppe* (fish soup), *fiskekaker* (fish cakes), *fiskeboller* (fish balls), and *fiskepudding* (fish pudding) on many menus. At the fish market, stalls feature shrimp and salmon served on a baguette with mayonnaise and cucumber. If you have a sweet tooth, don't miss *sommerbolle* (a cinnamon roll with a custard filling). In the summer, the harbor is lined with outdoor cafes. Also on the harbor is an **indoor food hall**. Following are a few suggestions for dining in Bergen.

Enhjørningen
One of the top seafood restaurants in Norway is housed in an old wooden building. Elegant and very expensive. The menu changes according to the day's catch. It's known for its *fiskesuppe* (fish soup) appetizer. If you're feeling adventurous, try the smoked whale! If you're not, dine on the *dampet kveite* (steamed halibut with parsley sauce).

Info: 29 Bryggen. Tel. 55 30 69 50. Reservations required. www.enhjorningen.no. Very Expensive.

Pingvinen
The name of this restaurant means "penguin." Want to try local specialties? This reasonably priced restaurant near the food hall serves everything from lamb dishes to fresh fish dishes. Try the Norwegian cheese platter.

Info: 14 Vasrerelven. Tel. 55 60 46 46. Open Mon-Thu 3:30pm-1am, Fri-Sun 1pm-1am. www.pingvinen.no. Moderate.

Trekroneren
Norwegian food on the run at this hot-dog stand (there is no seating). The hot dogs served here are huge and come in many varieties, including reindeer. Experiment with some traditional toppings such as lingonberry (mountain cranberry) and hot mustard. Perfect for a quick bite.

Info: 1 Kongs Oscars gate. No telephone. Inexpensive.

OSLO HOTELS

Expensive: over $200 (NOK1600)
Moderate: $100-$200 (NOK800 to NOK 1600)
Inexpensive: under $100 (NOK 800)

The Thief

This five-star hotel takes its name from its location on Tjuvholmen (Thieves Island). Modern and luxurious (it even features its own impressive art collection). Many rooms have views of the Oslofjord. Two restaurants and a spa add to the experience. 1 Landgangen. Tel. 24 00 40 00. www.thethief.com. Expensive.

Grand Hotel

The grand dame of Oslo's hotels opened in 1874. It's located in the city center and has every imaginable amenity (including indoor pool, spa, and fitness center). Fantastic location on the city's main street near some of the best restaurants and sights. The rooftop bar has memorable views and (expensive) cocktails. 31 Karls Johans gate. Tel. 23 21 20 00. www.grand.no. Expensive.

Hotel Continental

Opened in 1900, this award-winning hotel has a great location in the city center opposite the National Theater and near the Royal Palace. There are five restaurants and bars, including the famous Art-Nouveau Theatercaféen. 24/26 Stortingsgaten. Tel 22 82 40 00. www.hotelcontinental.no. Expensive.

Saga Hotel

This 47-room boutique hotel is located on a quiet residential street near the Royal Palace. The building housing the hotel dates back to the late 1800s. Each standard room includes television, coffee maker, and a minibar. 39 Eilert Sundits gate. Tel 22 55 44 90. www.sagahoteloslo.com. Moderate.

Thon Hotel Opera

This is *the* business hotel in Oslo with large conference facilities. Just a short walk from the central train station, the hotel also caters to tourists who appreciate its central location. Rooms include television, work desk, minibar, and free WiFi. The hotel restaurant offers great views of the Oslo Opera House. There's also a fitness center and bar. 4 Dronning Eufemias gate. Tel. 24 10 30 00. www.thonhotelsoslo.com. Moderate-Expensive.

Radisson Blu Plaza Hotel

This 37-story tower in the city center features views of the city's landmarks and the Oslofjord. The restaurant, bar, health club, and swimming pool all have panoramic views. 3 Sonia Henies plass. Tel. 22 05 80 00. www.radissonblu.com. Moderate.

Frogner House Apartments (Skovveien)

Our favorite place to stay in Oslo, these self-catering apartments are located in a Victorian-era building near the Royal Palace and a 15-minute walk from Frogner Park and the sculpture garden. All have kitchenettes and the added convenience of shared laundry for those on long trips. Many rooms have balconies. Frogner House Apartments also has several other locations throughout Oslo (see below). 8 Skovveien. Tel. 93 01 00 09. www.frognerhouse.no. Moderate.

Frogner House Apartments (Colbjørnsens gate)

This apartment/hotel is located in a renovated 19th-century town house near the Royal Palace. Televisions, kitchenettes, and free WiFi are some of the amenities offered here. An added bonus is that the hotel is located near the Nationaltheatret stop, the arrival and departure point for the Airport Express Train. 3 Colbjørnsens gate. Tel. 93 01 00 09. www.frognerhouse.no. Moderate.

Guldsmeden

Located near the waterfront, this 50-room hotel features four-poster beds and natural wood floors. The comfortable lobby and lounge features a fireplace and bar. If you want to relax after all that sightseeing, try the Turkish sauna. 78 Parkveien. Tel. 23 27 40 00. www.guldsmedenhotels.com/oslo. Moderate.

Comfort Hotel Karl Johan

Opened in 2016, this modern hotel is located on the city's main street near the Oslo Cathedral. A fantastic location and a great deal for budget travelers. Rooms are small, but include bathroom, flat-screen TV, and free WiFi. 12 Karl Johans gate. Tel. 23 01.03.50. www.nordicchoicehotels.com. Inexpensive-Moderate.

Cochs Pensjonat

Housed in an early-1900s building in central Oslo, this no-frills budget hotel provides free WiFi and rooms with private bathrooms and kitchenettes. Karl Johans Gate (the city's main street) is a 10-minute walk away. 25 Parkveien. Tel. 23 33 24 00. www.cochspensjonat.no. Inexpensive.

BERGEN HOTELS

Expensive: over $200 (NOK1600)
Moderate: $100-$200 (NOK800 to NOK 1600)
Inexpensive: under $100 (NOK 800)

Scandic Torget Bergen

This hotel has an excellent location overlooking the fish market and near the picturesque Bryggen wharf area in central Bergen. Rooms feature cable TV and a mini-bar. Huge breakfast buffet is included in the price. You can have a drink at the second-floor bar overlooking the water. 2-6 Strandkaien. Tel. 55.59.33.00. www.scandichotels.com. There are several other Scandic hotels in Bergen. Moderate.

Zander K

Located next to Bergen Train Station, this modern hotel features flat-screen TV, fitness room, wine bar, restaurant, and WiFi. An added bonus is the free use of bicycles so that you can pedal around town. 8 Zander Kaas gate. Tel. 55 36 20 40. www. zanderk.no. Moderate-Expensive.

First Hotel Marin

Centrally located in Bergen's Hanseatic harbor area, this comfortable hotel is only about a half-mile from both the train and bus stations. Each guest room has cable TV, work desk, free WiFi, gym, and sauna access. All rooms offer views of the street, courtyard, or mountains. Rooms on higher floors have harbor views. The airport express bus stops near here. The funicular and the Fish Market are both about a three-minute walk from the hotel. 8 Rosenkrantzgaten. Tel. 53 05 15 00. www.firsthotels.com. Moderate-Expensive.

Bergen Børs

Located in an elegant stock-exchange building from 1862, this hotel is convenient to nearby Bergen University and the aquarium. All rooms have a flat-screen TV, coffee machine, free WiFi, and mini-bar. There's also a bar, restaurant, and fitness center. 1 Vågsallmenningen. Tel. 55 33 64 00. www.bergen-bors.no. Expensive.

Budget Apartment Bergen Sekkegaten

Located near Bergen University, these basic apartments feature a small kitchen. Free WiFi. Popular with budget travelers. 2 Sekkegaten. www. budget-apartments.bergenhotelsweb.com. Inexpensive.

Det Hanseatiske Hotel

Old-world charm at this unique hotel located in a 16th-century building, next door to the Hanseatic Museum. It features rustic-style rooms with timber walls, wood furniture, and leather sofas. Most rooms have bathtubs and separate showers and free WiFi. The intimate Finnegårdsstuene Restaurant offers fine dining. The hotel is part the UNESCO World Heritage Bryggen district. The funicular is a two-minute walk away. 2A Finnegården. Tel. 55 30 48 00. www.dethanseatiskehotel.no/ Expensive.

Norway: Just the Facts

Location

The Kingdom of Norway is located in the western and northern parts of the Scandinavian Peninsula in northern Europe. Norway is bordered by Finland and Russia on the northeast and by Sweden on the east.

Cities

Oslo is the capital of Norway. With a population of approximately 600,000 people, it's Norway's largest city. Bergen is Norway's second-largest city with a population of nearly 300,000.

Geography

Norway covers 150,000 square miles. It's coastline is nearly 1700 miles long.

Population

Approximately five million.

Government

Norway is a unitary parliamentary democracy and a constitutional monarchy. It is governed by a king, prime minister, president, and chief justice. Norway has nineteen administrative counties known as *fylkers*.

Language
The official language is Norwegian, a North Germanic language. English is spoken fluently by nearly everyone.

Currency
The krone is the official currency of Norway. One krone is subdivided into 100 øre. It's abbreviated as NOK or kr. This book uses the abbreviation NOK.

Religion
The predominant religion in Norway is Christianity. Most Norwegians are Lutheran. Regular church attendance is among the lowest in Europe.

Economy
Norway is one of the wealthiest countries in the world, with extensive reserves of petroleum, natural gas, and minerals. It has the second-highest GDP per capita in the world.

National Holiday
Norway's Constitution Day is May 17.

Ethnicity
The vast majority of the Norwegian population is made up of Scandinavians of Germanic descent.

Latitude
From late May to late July, the sun never completely descends beneath the horizon in areas north of the Arctic Circle, and the rest of the country experiences up to 20 hours of daylight per day. From late November to late January, the sun never rises above the horizon in the north, and daylight hours are very short in the rest of the country.

7. PLANNING YOUR TRIP

GETTING AROUND OSLO

Arrivals

Clean and modern Oslo International Airport (OSL) www.osl.no is located at Gardermoen approximately, 50 km (30 miles) north of Oslo's Central City.

If you want to take a taxi from the airport, go to the taxi-information desk in the arrivals hall. They have information about the fixed rates and available taxis, so you'll have the option of choosing the cheapest one available. You don't need to take the first taxi at the taxi line. The average cost of a taxi from the airport to the central city of Oslo starts at an expensive NOK610.

The **Flytoget Airport Express Train** departs to and from Oslo S (Oslo Central Station) every 10 or 20 minutes. Duration to the airport is about 22 minutes. The cost is NOK198. *www.flytoget.no*.

The cheapest alternative is the local/regional train run by NSB. The airport train station is located within the terminal building. These trains are a good alternative for visitors going north (direction Lillehammer and Hamar) or further south (direction Tønsberg/Sandefjord/Skien). The trip is cheaper than the Airport Express to downtown Oslo. A single ticket costs NOK109. These trains will be marked with Drammen or Larvik (regional trains) or Kongsberg (local trains) in the direction towards Oslo, and they stop at Oslo Central Station (Oslo S). Travel time to Oslo Central Station is about 23 minutes. *www.nsb.no.*

The airport express train has more room for luggage than the local/regional trains.

Tickets for public transportation can be bought from the Public Transport desk or the N-Kiosk next to the exit from customs. You can also purchase tickets from machines or ticket desks at station entrances. Ticket machines are in both Norwegian and English. Tickets for the regional trains can also be bought online. The tickets usually need to be validated by reading machines at the entrance to the platforms. There are also 24-hour and seven-day passes available for all public transport in Oslo (*www.ruter.no*).

There are no local trains for the earliest and latest departures. You'll have to use the airport express train.

There are discounts for those over 67 and their partners (even if they are not over 67), and children under 16 travel free on weekends and some holidays.

Also located in front of the terminal is a bus line (Flybussen) which runs to Radisson Blu Scandinavia hotel via Oslo bus terminal every twenty minutes daily from 5:20am until 1:00am. Cost NOK189 single (NOK150 if bought on-line).

Car Rental
Avis, Hertz, Europcar, Budget and Sixt operate at Oslo Airport. The rental-car counters are located in the arrivals hall.

Taxis
Taxis are expensive in Norway. Only use taxis that display a special license. If you are taking a taxi from the airport, see the instructions above. In the city, prices begin at NOK100 and increase by NOK13.50 per kilometer. In Bergen, taxi fares begin at NOK75 and increase by NOK13 per kilometer.

Trains

Oslo's Central Station is linked to the rest of Europe through two cities in Sweden: Stockholm and Gothenburg. Stockholm is a five-hour trip, and Gothenburg is a three-hour trip. Norway's state railway is NSB. You can book at www.nsb.no. Sweden's state railway is SJ. You can book at www.sj.se.

PRACTICAL MATTERS

Banking & Changing Money

The krone (plural kroner) is the currency of Norway and is usually abbreviated as kr or NOK. It's subdivided into 100 øre, which exist only electronically since 2012. At the time of the printing of this book one krone equals .11 US dollars. One US dollar equals 9.17 kroner.

Call your credit-card company or bank before you leave to tell them that you'll be using your ATM or credit card outside the country. Many have automatic controls that can "freeze" your account if the computer program determines that there are charges outside your normal area. ATMs (with fees, of course) are the easiest way to change money in Norway. You'll find them everywhere, including the airport. Most ATMs have instructions in English. You can still get traveler's checks, but why bother? Beware that many establishments no longer accept them because of counterfeit checks.

Norway is one of the richest countries in the world and many things are very expensive (such as restaurants, taxis, and alcohol). Note that service and taxes Value Added Tax (VAT) is always included in the price. Hotel and restaurant prices are required by law to include taxes and service charges.

Norway is fast becoming a cashless society. You can pay for nearly anything with a credit card no matter how small the purchase.

Business Hours
Business hours are generally 8am-4pm Monday through Friday. Banks are open Monday through Friday, and some are open on Saturday mornings. Most shops are open 10am-5pm Monday through Friday and Saturday 9am-3pm. Some shops stay open later on Thursdays. Souvenir shops and shopping centers in tourist areas have extended hours.

Climate & Weather
Average high temperature/low temperature °C (°F)/days of rain or snow:

Oslo:
January: -2 (28)/-7 (19)/15
February: -1 (30)/-7 (19)/12
March: 4 (39)/-4 (25)/9
April 10: (50)/1 (34)/11
May: 16 (61)/6 (43)/10
June: 20 (68)/10 (50)/13
July: 22 (72)/13 (55)/15
August: 21 (70)/12 (54)/14
September: 16 (61)/8 (46)/14
October: 9 (48)/3 (37)/14
November: 3 (37)/-1 (30)/16
December: 0 (32)/ -4 (25)/17
Bergen:
January: 3 (37)/0 (32)/22
February: 4 (39)/0 (32)/19
March: 6 (43)/1 (34)/19
April 9: (48)/3 (37)/18
May: 14 (57)/7 (45)/17
June: 17 (63)/10 (50)/18
July: 18 (64)/12 (54)/19
August: 17 (63)/12 (54)/19
September: 14 (57)/9 (48)/20
October: 11 (52)/7 (45)/21
November: 7 (45)/3 (37)/21
December: 4 (39)/1 (34)/20

> ### Midnight Sun
>
> The midnight sun is a natural phenomenon found in latitudes north of the Arctic Circle, where the sun is visible at midnight. Depending on weather conditions, the sun is visible for 24 hours a day.
>
> The most popular location for travelers to experience the midnight sun is in Norway at the North Cape (Nordkapp).

Nearly half of Norway lies above the Arctic Circle, and is famous for the "midnight sun." It's dark for only a short time in summer.

You should check www.weather.com before you leave.

Consulates & Embassies
- US Embassy in Oslo: 36 Morgedalsvegen, Tel. 21308540 (emergency hot line). www.no.embassy.gov.
- Canadian Embassy in Oslo: 7 Wergelandsveien (4th floor), Tel. 22995300
- UK Embassy in Oslo: 8 Thomas Heftyes Gate, Tel. 23132700
- Australian citizens must contact the embassy in Denmark (+45)70263676, denmark.embassy.gov.au.

Electricity
The electrical current in Norway is 220 volts as opposed to 110 volts found in the U.S. and Canada. Don't fry your electric razor, hair dryer, or laptop. You'll need a converter and an adapter. Some laptops don't require a converter, but why are you bringing one anyway? You're on vacation, remember? Norway uses the europlug (type C & F), which has two round prongs.

Emergencies/Safety/Insurance
Don't wear a "fanny pack;" it's a sign that you're a tourist and an easy target (especially in crowded tourist areas). Avoid wearing expensive jewelry.

Check with your health-care provider. Most policies don't cover you overseas. If that's the case, you may want to obtain medical insurance. Given the uncertainties in today's world, you may also want to purchase trip-cancellation insurance (for insurance coverage, check out www.insuremytrip.com). Make sure that your policy covers sickness, disasters, bankruptcy and State Department travel restrictions and warnings. In other words, read the fine print!

Festivals & Holidays in Norway
- New Year's: January 1
- Maundy Thursday: movable date (Thursday before Easter)
- Good Friday: movable date (Friday before Easter)
- Easter: movable date
- Easter Monday: movable date (Monday after Easter)
- Labor Day: May 1
- Ascension Day: movable date (40 days after Easter)
- Constitution Day: May 17
- Pentecost: movable date (7th Monday after Easter)
- Christmas Eve: December 24
- Christmas: December 25
- St. Stephen's Day: December 26

Internet Access/WiFi
WiFi is available at most hotels, bars, cafes, and restaurants.

Language
Although, nearly everyone in Norway speaks fluent English, this book has included a list of some helpful Norwegian phrases. (It's always courteous to learn at least a few of them.)

Packing
Never pack prescription drugs, eyeglasses or valuables. Carry them on. Think black. It always works for men and women. And by the way, pack light. Don't ruin your trip by having to lug around huge suitcases. Before you leave home, make copies of your passport, airline tickets, and confirmation of hotel reservations. You should also make a list of your credit-card numbers and the telephone

LGBTQ

Norway was the second nation in the world to legalize same-sex partnerships (after the Netherlands). Norwegians were also on the forefront of legalizing same-sex marriage (in 2009).

Here are a few of the gay and gay-friendly establishments in Oslo:

London Pub, 5 C.J. Hambros plass: Friendly bar with a small terrace in the summer. Frequented by people of all ages. Fun karaoke nights! Tel 22 70 87 00. www.londonpub. no

Elsker, 9 Kristian IVs gate: Dance bar serving food. Tel. 45 25 60 42. www.elsker-oslo.no

So, 2 Arbeidergata 2: Popular lesbian bar. www.so-oslo.no

SLM Oslo, 28 Rådhusgata: Cruise club. www.slmoslo.no

Bob's Pub, 3 Grønland: Bar for mature men serving food with outdoor seating in the summer. Tel. 90 73 61 04. www. bobspub.no

César Bar & Café, 2 C.J. Hambros plass: Located next to the court house, this cafe and bar serves lunch and has live DJs on Fri and Sat nights. Tel. 47 91 01 35.

Saunahuset Hercules, 41 Storgata: Sauna. www.facebook. com/HerculesSauna/

Oslo Pride/Skeive Dager: Oslo's huge pride festival is held each June. www.oslopride.no

numbers for your credit-card companies. If you lose any of them (or they're stolen), you can call someone at home and have them provide the information to you. You should also pack copies of these documents separate from the originals.

Passport Regulations

Citizens of the United States who have been away more than 48 hours can bring home $800 of merchandise duty-free every 30 days. For more information, go to Traveler Information ("Know Before You Go") at www.cbp.gov. Canadians can bring back C$800 each year if gone for 48 hours or more. You'll need a valid passport to enter Norway from the United States and Canada for visits under three months. No visa is required.

Postal Services

Look for the "Posten" signs. The main post office is located at 7 Klingenberggata and is open Mon-Fri 7:30am-6pm, Sat 10am-3pm. Closed Sun. There are also small post-office stations in supermarkets. If you need a stamp, many souvenir shops sell them with postcards.

Restrooms

There aren't a lot of public restrooms. If you need to go, your best bet is to head (no pun intended) to the nearest café. It's considered good manners to purchase something if you use the restroom. There are some pay toilets that require NOK20-NOK50 to use. They're usually in places like Oslo Central Station.

Smoking

Smoking is prohibited in hotels, restaurants, bars, clubs, museums, and on public transportation. Smoking outdoors is also restricted in certain areas.

Telephones
- Country code for Norway: 47
- Calling Norway from the United States and Canada: Dial 011-47 plus the number listed in this book. There are no area codes in Norway.
- Calling the United States or Canada from Norway: Dial 00 (wait for the tone), dial 1 plus the area code and seven-digit local number
- Calling within Norway: Dial the number in this book

Phone cards purchased in Norway are the cheapest way to call. A great way to stay in touch and save money is to rent an international cell phone. One provider is www.cellhire.com. Not all cell phones purchased in the U.S. work in Europe. If you're a frequent visitor to Europe, you may want to purchase a cell phone (for about $50) from www.mobal.com. You'll get an international telephone number, and pay by the minute for calls made on the phone.

If you're using a smartphone in Norway, make sure to turn off your international roaming (and use WiFi instead) to save money.

Tipping
Restaurants automatically include a tax and service charge. Depending on the service, it's *sometimes* appropriate to leave up to 5%. Travelers from the U.S. sometimes have trouble not tipping. Remember, you do *not* have to tip.

It's customary, but not obligatory, to add a small tip or to round up. When you pay by credit card at a restaurant, the server will usually bring a mobile card reader and you have the option of stating the total (including any tip).

Service charges are added to most bills in Norway. Room service usually includes a service charge in the bill, so tipping is discretionary. Round up your taxi fare to the next round digit.

Tourist Information
The helpful tourist information center in Oslo is located right outside Central Station at the Oslo Visitor Centre. *Info*: 1 Jernbanetorget. Tel. 23 10 62 00. Open Jan-Mar and Oct-Dec Mon-Sat 9am-5pm, Sun 10am-4pm. Apr Mon-Sat 9am-6pm, Sun 10am-4pm. May-Jun and Sep daily 9am-6pm. Jul-Aug Mon-Sat 8am-7pm, Sun 9am-6pm. wwwvisitoslo.com.

Oslo Pass
The Oslo Pass gives you free entry to 30 museums and attractions in and around Oslo. It also includes free public transportation, discounts on concerts, restaurants and shops, along with plenty of ski-related discounts.

The cost for the pass in 2020 (with discounts for children and seniors) is: 24 hours: NOK 445, 48 hours: NOK 655, and 72 hours: NOK 820.

Water
Tap water is safe in Norway.

Web Sites
- Europe Made Easy Travel Guides: www.eatndrink.com
- Norway: www.visitnorway.com
- Oslo: www.visitoslo.com
- Bergen: www.visitbergen.com
- U.S. State Department: www.state.gov

PRONUNCIATION GUIDE

If you are looking for a comprehensive guide to speaking Norwegian, this is not the right place. What follows is simply a few tips for speaking Norwegian and a very brief pronunciation guide.

Remember that nearly everyone in Norway speaks fluent English.

A as in father
E as in bed
I as in beat
U as in food
Æ as in mad
Ø as in hurt
Å as in ball

Most consonants are pronounced similar to English, with some exceptions:

J is pronounced like the "y" in yes
R is a little more "rolled" than the English R

Special Norwegian pronunciations:
KJ, **KI** and **KY** make a soft k-sound without actually blocking the throat, so that the air makes a sound as it squeezes out
SJ, **SKY**, **SKJ** and **SKI** as in shop

ESSENTIAL PHRASES

Yes Ja
No Nei
Thank you Takk
Thank you very much Tusen takk
You're welcome Vær så god
Please Vær så snill
Excuse me Unnskyld meg
Hello Hallo
Goodbye Ha det

I do not understand Jeg forstår ikke

How do you say this in Norwegian? Hvordan sier man dette på norsk?

Where is ...? Hvor er ...?

How much is the fare? Hvor mye koster billetten?

One ticket to ..., please. En billett til ..., takk.

one en
two to
three tre
four fire
five fem
six seks
seven sju
eight åtte
nine ni
ten ti

Today I dag
Yesterday I går
Tomorrow I morgen

Train Tog
Bus station Busstasjon
Bus Buss
Bus station Busstasjon
Subway T-bane
Airport Flyplass
Bus station Busstasjon

Are there any vacancies for tonight? Er det noe ledig for i natt?
No vacancies Alt opptatt.

How much does this cost? Hvor mye koster dette?
What is this? Hva er dette?
I would like to buy ... Jeg vil gjerne ha ...
Do you have ... Har du ...
Do you accept credit cards? Tar dere kredittkort?

Tourist Information Turistinformasjon
Restrooms Toalett
Museum Museum
Bank Bank
Police station Politistasjon
Hospital Sykehus
Store/Shop Butikk
Restaurant Restaurant
Church Kirke

Day Dag
Week Uke
Month Måned
Year År
Monday mandag
Tuesday tirsdag
Wednesday onsdag
Thursday torsdag
Friday fredag
Saturday lørdag
Sunday søndag

THE CUISINE OF NORWAY

Norway isn't known for its cuisine. But, arrive here with an open mind and experience some interesting local specialties. Here are a few:

bløtkake, cream cake with fruit
brun saus, rich gravy
fenalår, mutton smoked, salted, and dried
fiskeboller, fish balls
fiskekabaret, shrimp, fish, and vegetables in gelatin
fiskesuppe, fish soup.
flatbrød, flat unleavened bread (made of wheat and barley)
fløtelapper, pancakes made with cream and served with sugar and jam
frukt saus, thickened fruit sauce
gammelost, hard, pungent cheese
geitost/gjetost, slightly sweet goat's cheese
gravetlaks, salmon marinated in sugar, salt, dill, and brandy
havrekjeks, oatmeal biscuits
juleskinke, marinated boiled ham
kjøttkaker med, burger with cabbage and a sweet and sour sauce
knekkebrød, crisp bread
koldtbord, buffet with cold meats, salads, herring, bread, and soup
kransekake, cake made with almonds, eggs, and sugar
lapskaus, meat (usually pork and/or venison) and vegetable stew
lomper, soft flatbread made with cooked potatoes and a bit of flour. Sort of a Norwegian tortilla
lutefisk, whitefish (usually cod) that has been air-dried and salted
multer, cloudberries (wild berries in the Arctic Circle)
mysost, cheese made from cow's milk.
nedlagtsild, marinated herring

pinnekjøtt, smoked mutton steamed over birch bark and served
    with cabbage
reinsdyrstek, reindeer steak
rekesalat, shrimp salad with mayonnaise
riskrem, rice pudding with whipped cream and sugar
spekemat, various types of smoked, dried meat
tilslørtbondepiker, stewed apples and breadcrumbs, served
    with cream
trollkrem, beaten egg whites (or whipped cream) and sugar
    mixed with cloudberries
trondhjemsuppea, milk broth with raisins, rice, sugar, and
    cinnamon
vafle, waffles

RESTAURANT PRICES IN THIS BOOK

Restaurant prices in this book are for a main course.

- Very Expensive: over NOK240
- Expensive: NOK160-NOK240
- Moderate: NOK80-NOK160
- Inexpensive: under NOK 80

8. INDEX

Europe Made Easy Travel Guides

Eating & Drinking Guides
Menu Translators and Restaurant Guides

- *Eating & Drinking in Paris*
- *Eating & Drinking in Italian*
- *Eating & Drinking in Spain and Portugal*
- *Eating & Drinking in Latin America*

Europe Made Easy Travel Guides

- *Amsterdam Made Easy*
- *Barcelona Made Easy*
- *Berlin Made Easy*
- *Europe Made Easy*
- *French Riviera Made Easy*
- *Italy Made Easy*
- *Oslo Made Easy*
- *Paris Made Easy*
- *Paris Walks*
- *Provence Made Easy*
- *Paris Travel Journal*
- *Italy Travel Journal*

For a list of all Europe Made Easy travel guides, and to purchase our books, visit www.eatndrink.com

www.ingramcontent.com/pod-product-compliance
Lightning Source LLC
Chambersburg PA
CBHW071536150726
48000CB00002B/812